FOUR PLAYS

Günter Grass

Four Plays

Flood

Onkel, Onkel

Only Ten Minutes to Buffalo

The Wicked Cooks

Introduction by Martin Esslin

London
Secker & Warburg

First published in England 1968 by
Martin Secker & Warburg Limited
14 Carlisle Street, London, W.1.

SBN : 436 18785 X

PRINTED PHOTOLITHO IN GREAT BRITAIN
BY EBENEZER BAYLIS AND SON, LIMITED
THE TRINITY PRESS, WORCESTER, AND LONDON

Contents

Introduction

If, almost a hundred years ago, Walter Pater could sum up the then prevailing trend in his famous epigram, "All art constantly aspires towards the condition of music," the dominant tendency of our own age might be described as an aspiration of all the arts to attain the condition of *images*. Even our music is said to be fully comprehensible only to those who, on hearing it, can *see* the symmetry and logic of its visual impact in the score; and certainly the contemporary novel tends toward a mosaic of strongly imagined snapshot images; and so also does the theater of our day. Günter Grass, the novelist and the playwright, provides a perfect illustration of this tendency. For Grass, the grocer's son from Danzig, called to the colors at the age of seventeen, released from an American prisoner-of-war camp at nineteen, working as an agricultural laborer and potash miner at twenty, found his vocation when he decided to become a visual artist and sought entry to the Düsseldorf Academy of Fine Arts. While waiting to gain admittance to that institution, he earned his living as a stonemason's apprentice and spent his time carving tombstones. He became a painter and sculptor of great promise and lived in Paris for some time among a cosmopolitan group of artists. As a writer Grass has remained a maker of images. His first published book, a slim volume of poems which appeared in 1956, is illustrated by his own spindly, fantasticated, semi-abstract drawings, and it is hard to tell whether the poems are there to illustrate the drawings, or the drawings to illustrate the poems.

Music has continuity, structure, harmony; that is why the art of happier, more settled, more secure epochs could aspire to the condition of music, a world of perfect transparency of meaning, a world that made sense. But a child of our time, like Grass, has seen the world move forward in a series of grotesque jerks, the frenzies of nationalism collapsing into national degradation, his native Danzig changing its status three times within seven years, starvation obscenely alternating with affluence; to such a child of our time life no longer moves along as a harmonious and logical progression; for such an observer the linking, logical structure has departed and what is left is a series of abrupt, changing, grotesque, incongruous, incoherent, but painfully vivid images, sordid, sad, yet so monstrous that one can only laugh about them:

> In our museum—we always go there on Sundays—
> they have opened a new department.
> Our aborted children, pale, serious embryos,
> sit there in plain glass jars
> and worry about their parents' future.

This short poem from his first collection sums up Grass's world with its peculiar mixture of disgust and black humor compressed into the capsule of a highly concentrated image.

The plays in this volume are essentially images seen with the eyes of a painter who is so obsessed with his images that they also seek expression as poetic metaphors; a lyrical poet so eager to see his metaphors come to life that he was compelled to write for the stage. Or to put it differently: so vivid were the images in the painter's, the poet's mind, that they had to start to talk in dialogue.

Grass himself, when questioned some years ago about his development as an artist, put it like this: "Up to now I have written poems, plays, and prose; all three types of writing are, in my case, based on dialogue, even the poetry. And so the transition from poetry to drama happened like this: poems were written in dialogue form, and were then extended. That was shortly after the war. Then slowly, gradually, stage directions were added, and so, parallel with my main occupation at that time, sculpture, I evolved my first play. That is why in a relatively short time, between

1954 and 1957, I wrote four full-length and two one-act plays, which, just like my poems and my prose, contain fantastic and realistic elements; these fantastic and realistic elements rub against each other and keep each other in check. . . ."

The genesis of the plays from the poems can be seen in one or two cases from Grass's volumes of poetry: in his first collection there is a poem entitled "Flood" which clearly contains the germ of the play:

> The cellar is submerged, we brought the crates up
> and are checking their contents against the list.
> So far nothing has been lost.
> Because the water is now certain to drop soon,
> we have begun to sew sunshades.
> It will be difficult to cross the square once more,
> distinct, with a shadow heavy as lead.
> We shall miss the curtain at first,
> and go into the cellar often
> to consider the mark
> which the water bequeathed us.

And in Grass's second volume of poems, published in 1960, there is a highly characteristic drawing of a cook swinging a spoon, which illustrates a poem about cooks and spoons:

> And some will say: a chef's a chef.
> All newly laundered, starched and spry
> in snowfall or against a wall
> that's whitewashed, chefs escape the eye
> and then the spoons they hold are all
> that stirs us, leaves us in no doubt:
> the things we eat, the chefs dish out.

Indeed, in Grass's world the cooks, in their white uniforms, play a part second only to that of the nuns in their black habits. No wonder that the cooks also carry a metaphysical significance in Grass's world. "I like cooking," he once confessed in an interview, "I like cooking lentils, for example. Lentils and luck have a great deal in common for me." And so the cooks, who feed us all, can become images of man's quest for spiritual as well as physical nourishment.

There is an overwhelming, childlike directness and simplicity in the way in which the most earthy and concrete things—lentils, food, nourishment—are here equated with the sphere of the spiritual, the philosophical, the metaphysical abstraction—happiness, the meaning of life. It is the simplicity of the medieval craftsmen who carved the gargoyles that adorn the great cathedrals. And it is characteristic of Grass, the stonecarver, the sculptor, the painter and maker of images. Grass's subject matter, the degradation of Germany in the time of Hitler and in the aftermath of war, is sordid and disgusting in the extreme. And in his writings—poems, plays, and novels—he never tries to evade the most direct confrontation with all these nauseating facts. But because he deals with them so directly, with the total lack of self-consciousness, the innocence of a child, the disgusting facts can be accepted without the physical reactions of disgust which would make them intolerable as the subject matter of an artist's vision. If Brecht spoke of naïveté as one of the most precious of aesthetic categories, Grass possesses that innocence of vision to a degree unparalleled by any other writer of our time.

It is the vision of a Douanier Rousseau, a Paul Klee. And Grass's plays can best be seen as images from that sphere brought to life on a three-dimensional canvas; the house with its inmates and its rats with the waters rising and receding in *Flood (Hochwasser,* first performed in Frankfurt, 1957) ; the rusty engine stationary in an idyllic landscape, manned by a crew using nautical language, who delude themselves that they are driving along at top speed, in *Only Ten Minutes to Buffalo* * (*Noch zehn Minuten bis*

---

* The title of this play requires some explanation: *Und noch zehn Minuten bis Buffalo* is a line from a poem by Theodor Fontane (1819-1898) entitled "John Maynard." This tells the story of a ship bound from Detroit to Buffalo on Lake Erie, which bursts into flame half an hour before it is due to dock at Buffalo. Surrounded by flames, the heroic helmsman, John Maynard, remains at his post and steers the

Buffalo, first performed in Berlin, 1959) ; the series of images of the pedantic murderer Bollin, trying to fulfill his duty as a member of a murderous generation, and always foiled, in *Onkel, Onkel* (first performed in Cologne, 1958); and the image of the cooks—which Grass first used in a ballet—*Fünf Köche* (performed at Aix-les-Bains and Bonn in 1959) —clinically white in their uniforms, professionals angry to see that the highest secret of their art eludes them, while an amateur gains effortless possession of it, in *The Wicked Cooks* (*Die bösen Köche,* first performed in Berlin, 1962) .

None of these plays has, as yet, achieved a lasting success in the theater. It has been said that Grass's dramatic works lack the documentary quality, the descriptive, autobiographical detail which he incorporates in his novels. But this, to me, seems to overlook the essential difference between the narrative and the dramatic form. If Grass wrote plays filled with details about his early years in Danzig he would be producing naturalistic drama wholly at variance with his own artistic personality. In the novels it was possible to combine the most abundant autobiographical detail with the wildest flights of grotesque fantasy. There is no time in drama to preserve both of these elements. Yet, precisely because the dramatic form demands more conciseness, more concentration, because it makes Grass confine himself to a limited number of images in each of his plays, it brings out his lyrical quality, the quality of his vision as a carver of images. Nor is it a coincidence that each of his long novels contains passages written in dialogue and, indeed, that these dialogue passages could be performed in the theater: the episode of the nuns on the Atlantic Wall from *The Tin Drum* was staged in Düsseldorf; the discussion chapter from *Dog Years* at Munich.

Indeed, for a writer of Grass's chaotic and anarchic ex-

---

ship into port, saving the passengers' lives while himself dying a hero's death. This poem, which is much read in German schools, is thus the German equivalent to "Casabianca" (*"The boy stood on the burning deck"*), and, for Grass, the epitome of bombastic, nautical nonsense.

uberance as a storyteller the dramatic form provides a most
salutary discipline; on the other hand, the dramatist is to
a much greater degree in the hands of his directors and per-
formers. The relative lack of success in the theater of the
plays in this volume may well be due to the difficulty of
finding the right style for their performance. Grass himself
has criticized the timidity of managements in Germany in
tackling unusual works like his own plays. And there certainly is some substance in these strictures. His latest play,
The Plebeians Rehearse the Uprising, has caused a much
greater stir; but here the more topical—and more sensa-
tional—subject matter played its part; for here Grass
showed a playwright and producer in East Berlin rehears-
ing *Coriolanus* on 17 June 1953 while the real rising takes
place in the streets outside the theater. The identification
of the playwright with Brecht imposed itself and the German press relished the opportunity of showing a leading
writer of a younger generation attacking the dominant personality of an earlier period. And yet, the real subject matter of the play lies at a far deeper level: Grass's concern
was not to score a point against Brecht but to show the
dilemma of the creative artist in his relationship with politi-
cal authority. Here too he had found a powerful image
which admirably summed up and compressed a complex
state of affairs into a simple and telling metaphor.

Günter Grass is a committed writer; it is one of the most
hopeful signs for the future of Germany that her leading
literary figures have broken with a long-standing tradition
that artists of all kinds should keep aloof from politics.
However fantastic and unrealistic the plays in this volume
may appear at first sight, here too the social comment is
present and very much to the fore: in *Flood* there is a powerful warning against any nostalgia for the times of calamity
and camaraderie; the murderer in *Onkel, Onkel* and the
murderous teen-agers have obvious implications for mem-
bers of both generations in present-day Germany; in *The
Wicked Cooks* there are clear reflections of power struggles
and intrigues; and even the slight parodistic curtain-raiser

Only Ten Minutes to Buffalo can, ultimately, be seen as an attack against illusions, a plea for realism in looking at the contemporary scene. There is thus no split between Grass, the author of seemingly abstruse, absurdist plays, and Grass the indefatigable campaigner for the Social Democratic Party in the German elections of 1965.

> Whoever wishes
> to release, to breathe out
> that caries which long has lurked behind the toothpaste
> has no choice but to open his mouth.
>
> Now let us open our mouths,
> go to offices and hand in
> the bad gold teeth
> which we broke and plucked from the dead.
>
> Before you can hope to
> displace, to spew out fat fathers—
> now that we too are fathers and putting on fat—
> you've no choice but to open your mouths;
>
> just as our children in time will
> open their mouths, will displace,
> will spew out the great caries,
> the bad gold teeth, the fat fathers.

Only if we understand that this is the impulse behind everything that Günter Grass writes are we in a position to appreciate his poems, his novels, and his plays.

MARTIN ESSLIN

The poetry quoted above has been taken from *Selected Poems*, translated by Michael Hamburger and Christopher Middleton (New York and London, 1966).

Flood

A Play in Two Acts

Translated by Ralph Manheim

Cast of Characters

NOAH, the owner of the house

BETTY, his sister-in-law

YETTA, his daughter

HENRY, Yetta's fiancé

LEO, Noah's son

CONGO, Leo's friend

THE INSPECTOR

PEARL and POINT, two rats

Act I

(*A house in cross section, showing the cellar stairs, a room with a low ceiling, a flat roof with chimney.*

The cellar stairs are littered with candelabra, photograph albums, and loose photographs. NOAH *is trying, with* BETTY's *help, to move a large crate up the stairs. The room and roof are in half darkness*)

BETTY:

We're going to catch our death of cold.

NOAH:

It has to be done, Betty. It's indispensable, in . . .

BETTY:

I know, I know. But most of your collection is upstairs already. Really, I . . .

NOAH:

Just this one little crate.

BETTY:

I'm perfectly willing, brother dear, but it's just too heavy.

NOAH:

Some of the Burgundian pieces are sure to be in it. Those are the very rarest.

BETTY:

How do you know? There's no way of knowing. Goodness only knows what might be in it. (*She leafs through a photograph album*) Oh, Noah, look at this picture of Leo.

NOAH:

Leo, Leo—hm. But what about those parasites upstairs? Why don't they come down and help?

BETTY:

What a Handsome child he was! And so clever! So lively!
Do you remember the time when you and I and Erna . . .

NOAH:

My wife wasn't there. She never was.

BETTY:

Well, maybe not. She was kind of ailing even then. Anyway, it was on the beach at Steegen. Suddenly the little
fellow begins to stare at a lady. She had on a blue-and-red
striped bathing suit. And do you remember what he . . .

NOAH:

Betty! Can't you see that this is no time or place to . . .
they've got to come and help. Yoo-hoo.

BETTY:

I doubt if they can hear you.

NOAH:

They don't want to. All they ever do is lie around mis-
behaving.

BETTY:

You're too hard on them. They're still young. It's mighty
chilly down here.

NOAH:

It's all going to be ruined. All my work. All these years
of toil, patience, self-abnegation. Half a lifetime. All my
travels. The mileage . . .

BETTY:

Yes, I'll hand it to you. You've worked hard at it. And
what for? For inkwells. Little ones, big ones, thin ones,
fat ones. And some of them are cracked.

NOAH:

I wouldn't expect you to understand.—Here, look at this
one. You can still see a trace of violet ink. Yes, I know,
it's dry and hard now. But do you know who dipped a
pen into this exquisite inkwell? Queen Louise on her way
into exile. She spent the night here and wrote several
letters . . .

BETTY:

But they say . . .

NOAH:

Yes, I know. They say it was only personal letters and that
she tore them up the same night. Maybe so. But what
difference does that make? She was a real queen.

BETTY:

Yes, that she was.

NOAH:

We stand here gabbing and the water's rising.

BETTY:

Why, so it is. And it's chilly too. We'd better . . .

NOAH:

Why don't they come down? They only think of themselves. They've hauled up the phonograph records and a
lot of old magazines and the last case of beer.

BETTY:

And the preserving jars, Noah, you mustn't be unfair.

NOAH:

Unfair! I mustn't be unfair! Will you kindly tell me why?

BETTY:

Noah!

NOAH:

Does anyone ever ask about me? Does anyone ever give
me a hand? They lie up there multiplying, you spend the
time leafing through your silly albums and showing me
pictures of my children. Pictures. Let them come in person
and give me a hand. Yoo-hoo! Yoo-hoo!

BETTY:

Noah, you're going to have a stroke.

NOAH:

I'm sorry. Yes, I ought to think of my health.

BETTY:

Yes, you really should, my dear. You're not as young as
you used to be.

NOAH:

That's the truth. But why don't they come? They know everything's going to be ruined. The labels will come off. The ink will run.

BETTY:

You mustn't take it so hard. You can put on new ones later.

NOAH:

Later! Who knows what's going to happen later?

BETTY:

Who knows what's . . . What do you mean by that?

NOAH:

Well, my dear. We've all of us got to someday, don't we?

BETTY:

Noah!

NOAH:

You've got to expect the worst in life. (*Indicating the crates*) This is the only thing I ever relied on—my work. Yes, I know, it's not great. As you say, its nothing but inkwells. And yet it has its significance. It's my lifework. It must not have been in vain.—You see a broken man.

BETTY:

Why, Noah . . .

NOAH:

The water has been rising again since Monday. And those numskulls upstairs don't know a thing. They think rain is just a sound, a phonograph record with a crack in it, that keeps droning out the same old thing. And when you're sick of it, you just turn it off. You see what I mean? They think they can just turn the rain off when they've had enough of it.

BETTY:

Yes, I suppose so. I guess you're right.

NOAH:

Of course I'm right. We can't just leave them standing

here, everything would be ruined.—Maybe there are photographs in the crate too. In fact I'm sure of it. Pictures
of Leo, your angel.

BETTY:

Do you really think so? Here in this crate? In that case
there's no time to lose. We've got to . . . Children, children! Yoo-hoo! (*She claps her hands. It grows slowly dark
on the cellar stairs, while the light goes on in the room.
Grandfather clock and middle-class furniture, almost entirely submerged by crates, candelabra, and photograph
albums. In the right half of the room, where the view is
still clear,* HENRY *and* YETTA *are sitting on the bed*)

HENRY:

Yetta, your father's calling.

YETTA:

Let him call.

HENRY:

Don't you think I ought to have a look? Maybe something's wrong.

YETTA:

What can be wrong? They can come up if they want us.

HENRY:

Maybe I'd better take a quick look.

YETTA:

No. You stay right here and get started with your hocus-
pocus.

HENRY:

All right, if you want me to. But really, it's not hocus-
pocus. It really works. When it's finished, I'll be able to
tell you the exact number. But you must pay attention.

YETTA:

Okay, okay. Get started.

HENRY:

All right. Now watch me. Thumb.

YETTA:

Thumb.

HENRY:

No, you mustn't say anything.

YETTA:

Okay, okay.

HENRY:

Why are you so irritable?—Well, thumb, forefinger, middle finger, ring finger, little finger. Got it?

YETTA:

Mm.

HENRY:

Good. Now back again. Little finger, ring finger, skip two.

YETTA:

Why?

HENRY:

Because that's the way it goes. Just pay attention. Skip two. Now you've got to think of something.

YETTA:

Okay.

HENRY:

And a number that goes with it.

YETTA:

All right.

HENRY:

So now we start over from the beginning. Thumb . . .

YETTA:

Thumb.

HENRY:

Don't talk, pay attention.

YETTA:

Okay, damn it.

HENRY:

Pointer, middle finger, ring finger, little finger, fist. What did you think of?

YETTA:

I won't tell you.

HENRY:

But I've got to know if you want me to guess the number. Otherwise I can't . . .

YETTA:

I'm not in the mood.

HENRY:

Tell me!

YETTA:

Can't you guess? You're usually so clever about such things. A bright boy like you with such a father.—Say, why didn't you clear out with your old man when this thing started? You'd be high and dry by now. You wouldn't be here shivering.

HENRY:

I'm not shivering.—So tell me, what did you think of?

YETTA:

Is this really a game or are you just spying on me again? Didn't you say you could figure the whole thing out?

HENRY:

Yes, of course I can. But first I've got to know what you were thinking.

YETTA:

Well, I won't tell you.

HENRY:

Don't be a kill-joy.

YETTA:

There's no connection. I'm just not in the mood. That can happen, can't it?

HENRY:

All right, so you're not in the mood. But suppose I say pretty please.

YETTA:

Aw, forget it.

HENRY:

But I, I love you.

YETTA:

I know, I know. Everybody knows. If the newspapers were still coming out, it would be on the front page.

HENRY:

Tell me.

YETTA:

No.

HENRY:

All right, then I'll guess.

YETTA:

Go ahead.

HENRY:

You thought about me.

YETTA:

Don't make me laugh.

HENRY:

Then you thought about . . . about this morning.

YETTA:

This morning?

HENRY:

You thought you might be pregnant, because . . .

YETTA:

Rot.

HENRY:

Then tell me.

YETTA:

Does it interest you so much? I don't see why!

HENRY:

But it does. (*He stands up. With restrained emotion*) I'll always ask. I've got to know everything you think, every single thing.—When you stand here looking in the mirror, you don't really look in the mirror, you just look

through it; or when you tap your fingers on the table or
bite into an apple, or when you don't do anything at all,
when you're just there—I always wonder what you're
thinking. When you go to the closet, what are you thinking, when you put on your sweater, always the same faded
old rag, what are you thinking? Out with it. What did
you think about?

(HENRY *sits down,* YETTA *stands up slowly and goes to the
window*)

YETTA:

Here's what I thought: How long is it going to keep on
raining and what's rain anyway? I see lines running from
top to bottom, or maybe it's the other way around. I can't
tell the difference any more.

HENRY:

You thought more than that.

YETTA (*turns slowly toward* HENRY):

I thought: How high will the water have to rise to make
you shut up? Take it from me. Before you'll ever get
anywhere, you'll have to hit rock bottom. (YETTA *goes
back to bed*) I'm going to lie down. Why shouldn't I lie
down? Does it change anything for me to stand in front
of—or behind—this damned curtain—so cold, so wet?

HENRY:

Can I lie down beside you?

YETTA:

No, you never lie still.

HENRY:

You used to sing a different tune. Those three weeks by
the lake, you couldn't get enough.

YETTA:

Yes. But that was different.

HENRY:

What do you mean? Don't you care for me any more?

YETTA (*starts up*):

Sh-sh. Don't you hear something? On the roof?

HENRY:

No. Really. Not a thing. (*Dramatically*) I only hear my blood, I always hear my blood, and when I . . .

YETTA:

Shit on your blood.—There's something squeaking up there. I can hear it plain as day. Man, there *is* somebody up there. (*She jumps up*)

HENRY:

It's only the rats. They were in the cellar before, now they're on the roof.

(*It slowly grows dark in the room and light on the roof. Two large, grotesquely disheveled rat masks are sitting on the edge of the roof*)

PEARL:

I'm beginning to feel like a bird.

POINT:

Except you can't sing yet.

PEARL:

That will come. If this goes on, I'll begin to lay eggs and brood.

POINT:

Damn it all. The stuff looks like string. I'd like to bite into it.

PEARL:

Bite away if you feel like it. But don't swallow, or you'll get a tapeworm.

POINT:

That's all I need. I only wish I knew . . .

PEARL:

What's going to become of us. So would I. We're not water rats after all. Maybe we'll have to climb up on the chimney.

POINT:

That wouldn't be so bad. By that time it won't be smoking any more.

PEARL:

I wonder where the others are now. They always thought they knew better. Such things don't happen nowadays. That's what they said.

POINT:

Snout floated by a little while ago. He looked all worn out. (*Worried*) I'd just like to know . . .

PEARL:

What is it now?

POINT:

. . . if there are any sparrows up here.

PEARL:

Why, you want to take flying lessons?

POINT:

No, not exactly. But . . .

PEARL:

Well, then, why worry about sparrows? (POINT *scurries anxiously back and forth*)

POINT:

Come on, Pearl, let's get out of here.

PEARL:

But where can we go?

POINT:

Where it's more protected. There, behind the chimney.

PEARL:

Are you out of your mind? You want to multiply up here, on the roof?

POINT:

Come along, Pearl. Come along. (POINT *and* PEARL *disappear behind the chimney*)

(*The light goes out on the roof. The room becomes bright.* YETTA *is lying on the bed;* HENRY *near her on a chair, turning his back to her*)

YETTA:

Sometimes I think we're floating. Then I think, watch out, now there's going to be a jerk, and we'll be there. No matter where, someplace nice. Java or someplace.

HENRY:

Or dead. That's not bad either.

YETTA:

Cut it out. Dead people are foreigners. We don't understand what they say.

HENRY:

Hm.

YETTA (*sits up*):

Would you like to lie down? Henry, I asked you a question.

HENRY:

You always reel it off so simply. And when you're done, you think it's right.

YETTA:

What?

HENRY:

Like just now. About death and all that.

YETTA:

Cut the shit. You started it.

HENRY:

Maybe you're right.

YETTA:

I'll say. Well, how about it? Are you coming or not?

HENRY:

Forget it. I'm fine right here.

YETTA:

Okay.

HENRY:

But I can lie down anyway if you want me too.

(*As* HENRY *takes off his jacket and approaches the bed, the room darkens and the stairs are lighted.* NOAH *tug-*

ging at the crate, BETTY *leafing through a photograph album*)

BETTY:

I've always been crazy about this picture of him. He's kind of laughing and looks like a real boy.

NOAH:

Yes, he didn't laugh very often.

BETTY:

That's so. He was a serious child—but so clever.

NOAH:

Clever, you say, hm, wouldn't you say he was a little sneaky too, a little false, or . . . maybe just plain rotten to the core?

BETTY:

Noah, how **can you** . . . ?

NOAH:

I know what you're going to say, he's my son, that's what you're going to say. Good, he's still my son, but wasn't he my son when he ran up debts in my name? And what about the scandal in the hospital?

BETTY:

You just kept too tight a hold on him, Noah. You were too strict. A child like Leo needed tenderness. While Erna was alive . . .

NOAH:

She couldn't manage him either. She was always complaining about him and weeping on my shoulder, but what's the use of talking? He left us. He made his bed.

BETTY:

And suppose he comes back all of a sudden?

NOAH:

Look. In another minute the crate will be in the water. Let's try again. We've got to, Betty.

BETTY:

But it's hopeless. You know it's hopeless.

NOAH:

I'd better call them again. What do you think?

BETTY:

In this rain? Nobody'll hear you.

NOAH:

Yetta, Yetta, tell your boy friend to come down and help me.

BETTY:

I told you nobody could hear you in this rain. But of course you'd have to try. Let's break the crate open. Tools? Here are the tools.

NOAH:

You're right. I'll have to break it open. (*He takes a hammer and crowbar and starts to open the crate*) We'll take them up piece by piece.

BETTY:

Oh, maybe there's another album in it. Wouldn't that be nice!

NOAH:

It's perfectly possible, my dear, perfectly possible. Oof. That does it. Jumping Jehosaphat! (LEO *and his friend* CONGO *step out of the crate. They are wearing faded khakis, rather resembling uniforms*)

LEO:

Europe! It's cooler here. Quite a lot cooler. Hiya, Pop, long time no see. This here is Congo. This is my old man. Archibald Noah, collector of inkwells and candelabras. What do you say, Congo, did I promise too much?

CONGO:

I am delighted to make your acquaintance, Munseer Noah. Inkwells. Not bad. It's kind of a change.

BETTY:

Is it really you?

LEO:

Aunt Betty! Well, I'll be . . .

BETTY:

Yes, indeed. It's your old Aunt Betty. Let's have a look at you, boy. Can it really be? I was just saying to your father, wasn't I, Noah, I was just saying, just now, only a moment ago, maybe there's a snapshot of Leo in there.

LEO:

Aunt Betty! The long-playing record! Nothing can stop her.

BETTY:

Why, Leo!—And this is your friend. A splendid-looking young man.—Noah, what do you say?

NOAH:

I . . . I can't believe it.

LEO:

What's that? Surprised? You made a little mistake, that's all. You picked the wrong crate. Take a look. No sign of any Burgundian inkwells. You know what's in there? Tonkin and Laos, the screwed-up kingdom. (*He pushes* NOAH *to the crate*) Go on, Pop, take a look. Get a whiff of jungle.

NOAH:

Stop that, Leo. Have you forgotten . . .

LEO:

What? That you're my Pop? Well, yes, I really did kind of forget out there. But I got to give you credit. You're still my Pop all right, same as ever. You haven't changed a bit.

BETTY:

But you have, Leo. Goodness, how you've changed. How big and strong you are!

LEO:

Aunt Betty and her bun! Look how it wobbles. Man! And still the same old photograph album on her lap.

NOAH:

Leo, your friend . . .

LEO:

You can talk to him direct. He don't bite.

NOAH:

Mr. . . . ?

CONGO:

Congo's my name.

LEO:

He used to be a boxer.

CONGO:

Turn it off.

NOAH:

Mr. Congo, unless I am very much mistaken, I have heard of you. Aren't you the young gentleman who once persuaded my son to go to the Rhineland, where he . . . I trust you know what I'm referring to.

CONGO:

Sure thing, that was me. Unless I'm very much mistaken, you are referring to our little Sunday excursion. Sure, I know, it took a little longer than we planned. But now we're back again, aren't we?

LEO:

And how! Don't take it so hard, Pop.

NOAH:

Well, well, so here you are. A hearty welcome, yes, yes, a hearty welcome.

BETTY:

I should say so. A hearty welcome! Oh, won't Yetta be pleased!

LEO:

Is she here?

NOAH:

Yes, my daughter Yetta is here, she stuck by her father. —I don't know exactly how to put it. Don't get me wrong. But I'm sorry to say, my dear Leo, hm . . . that you've come at a rather unfortunate time.

LEO:

No kidding?

NOAH:

Let me repeat: don't misunderstand me . . .

LEO:

Spit it out.

NOAH:

My dear Leo, we are having a flood. Don't you see what that means? You must believe me, Mr. Congo. At the moment all four of us are suffering from the effects of a disastrous flood. It is to be feared . . .

LEO:

All four? What do you mean? Is somebody else here?

NOAH:

I'm afraid so. Yetta's fiancé.

LEO:

Yetta's fiancé?

BETTY:

Yes. Henry. You don't know him.

LEO:

What's his name again?

BETTY:

Henry—isn't it a nice name? He's a nice boy, too. Kind of skinny and jumpity, but that will pass in time. Besides, he loves her.

LEO:

Does he say so?

BETTY:

What's that?

LEO:

Does he say he loves her and all that stuff?

BETTY:

He keeps telling her over and over.

LEO:

Maybe it's true if he says it so often. Yetta and her fiancé, get a load of that. Only a couple of years ago she was playing doctor and patient in the yard with Nuchi and Axel. And now she's got a fiancé. Time passes, doesn't it, Congo?

CONGO:

Looks like it.

NOAH:

Well, as I was saying, my dear Leo, we haven't got much room. It's a downright shame, but unfortunately, we just haven't got . . .

LEO:

What, you want to put us out in the open? We drop in for a visit, we're friendly, we're polite, we're obliging, and you want to put us out in the open.

NOAH:

But.

BETTY:

But me no buts. We'll make room . . .   Won't Yetta be surprised!

NOAH:

Yes, yes, of course.

LEO:

Eh, Congo, what do you think of Aunt Betty? Isn't she a number? You go ahead and take the junk. Got everything?

CONGO:

I'm getting there.

NOAH:

I guess I'll take this. And maybe this.

BETTY:

I'm going to take the album. What do you think, Leo? Shouldn't I?

LEO:

Of course you should, Auntie. A woman without a picture album is like a coffin without a lid. (NOAH and BETTY *in the lead, all slowly climb the stairs.* CONGO *has a bundle under his arm. The light goes on in the room.* HENRY *sits up and puts on his jacket*)

HENRY:

Yetta, your father's coming.

YETTA:

Let him come. (*Turns to the wall*)

NOAH (*in the doorway*):

Yetta, angel, guess what I've got?

BETTY:

Oh yes, Yetta, guess, guess. (*Pushes past* NOAH *and rushes almost to the middle of the room*)

NOAH:

Something very special.

BETTY (*beaming*):

You'll be amazed.

YETTA:

I can imagine. (*Slowly sits up*) Either you've got a pile of your dopey inkwells or some idiotic family picture with everybody in it: the school principal in the middle, and up front the dear little children. Am I right?—Or Leo's here?

BETTY:

You've guessed it.

NOAH:

How did you know?

LEO (*pushes* NOAH *aside*):

Hiya, Yetta.

YETTA:

Hiya, Leo. You're back?

LEO:

Just dropped in. Thought we'd have a look-see. Say, you look pretty good, as far as I can see from here.

YETTA:

Why shouldn't I?

LEO:

This here is Congo, my friend. I want you to be nice to him. He hasn't got any father and mother.

YETTA:

I can think of worse calamities.—Hi.

CONGO:

I wish you a very good day, Mamzelle, I do hope we are not inconveniencing you.

LEO:

Don't talk so fancy—He used to be a boxer; that's why he gets so polite sometimes.

NOAH:

But Yetta, child, aren't you surprised that our Leo has found his way home after all these years?

BETTY:

Just think. All of a sudden he was here.

YETTA:

Surprised? Why? All along I've been saying: If it keeps on raining like this, Leo will come home. And look! Here he is.

BETTY:

Yes, Noah, honor bright. She really did say that about the rain.

NOAH:

Anyway, it's the truth. He always comes back in the worst kind of weather. (LEO *looks around the room*)

LEO:

Who's that over there?

YETTA:

Him?

LEO:

Yeah, him.

NOAH:

That's Henry, Yetta's fiancé; his father is an eminent physician. I hope you two will hit it off.

LEO:

I don't like doctors. The guy looks like a hairdresser.

YETTA:

Leave him alone. He hasn't done anything to you.

LEO:

Okay, okay. Well, Congo, how do you like it here? In my house?

CONGO:

Your sister . . .

LEO:

I didn't ask you about my sister. I asked you how you like it here. Real cute, ain't it?

CONGO:

Oh, the house you mean? Why, yes. What shall I say? Cozy, yes, cozy. Coziest place I ever saw.

LEO:

So you think it's cozy?

CONGO:

I'll say. When I look at that grandfather clock, a feeling of religion comes over me like when I was a kid. But about your sister . . .

LEO:

What about my sister?

CONGO:

Nothing. Just like that. She appeals to me. Do you know, she's got a certain something, I can't describe it.

LEO:

Never mind. It's all the same to me.

HENRY:

I gather that you have been away for some time?

LEO:

   Hey, he's talking to you.

CONGO:

   To me? If we've been away. Yep, you've gathered right—
We've been away a long time.

HENRY:

   And where have you been? That is to say, what places
have you visited, if I may ask.

LEO:

   Tell him no, he shouldn't ask.

CONGO:

   D'you hear that? Mustn't ask. Questions verboten! Ever
hear of Lohengrin? See?

YETTA:

   Yeah, shut your trap.

LEO:

   Hey, Congo, let's see the bundle.

CONGO:

   It didn't even get very wet.

LEO (*opens the bundle and takes out a long strip of white
   silk*):

   Betty, my goldfish, see what I've got here.

BETTY:

   Heavens above, can it be? Where on earth did you get it?

LEO:

   It's yours, we brought it for you. It's first-class parachute
silk. Eh, Congo?

CONGO:

   It sure is.

BETTY:

   No, I can't believe it. Parachute silk! It's too wonderful. I
can't accept it. What do you think, Noah?

NOAH:

   Don't ask me. I am in no position to judge whether this
silk . . .

BETTY:

Parachute silk.

NOAH:

Very well. Whether this parachute silk was acquired by proper legal methods or . . .

YETTA:

Stow it! You always have to put in your two cents' worth. Do you want to spoil Auntie's fun?

HENRY:

I'm sure there is nothing to worry about, Mr. Noah . . .

YETTA:

It's all right, Auntie. If Leo brings something, it's sure to be okay.

BETTY:

Do you really think so, Yetta? Well, in that case, thank you kindly. And you too, Mr. Congo.

CONGO:

It's nothing. Don't mention it. Glad to do it for a sweet old lady.

BETTY (*threatening him with her forefinger*):

Oh, Mr. Congo! You sound so wicked!

LEO:

That's right, Auntie. Better watch your step with him.

BETTY:

No, really. And so much of it. Do you know what I'm going to make?

LEO:

What?

BETTY:

A little parasol for each one of you.

LEO:

No kidding?

BETTY:

Honest to goodness. Little parasols, one, two, three, four, five, and if there's any left, one for me too. Six little parasols.

YETTA:

You're rich, Auntie. It's raining cats and dogs and you talk about parasols.

BETTY:

A stitch in time, my dear. It won't rain forever.

NOAH:

You never can tell.

BETTY:

Nonsense. Don't you suppose the rain ever gets bored?

LEO:

She's perfectly right. When the rain's good and sick of it, the sun will come back.

YETTA:

Why are you always trying to be so smart? Take a rest. Or tell us something about your adventures.

LEO:

There's nothing to tell about.

YETTA:

Suits me.

(*The room slowly darkens. The light goes on on the roof*)

PEARL:

Tell me a little story, Point.

POINT:

Looks like they've got company downstairs.

PEARL:

I hadn't noticed. Go on, Point, tell me something.

POINT:

What?

PEARL:

Any old thing. You've had so many experiences. A well-traveled rat like you. Go on. Get started.

POINT:

Yes, I have seen a thing or two in my time. Should I tell you about the time I was in the safe for three days and there was nothing to eat but twenty-mark bills? Or would you rather hear the story about the clock?

PEARL:

What was that one?

POINT:

Well, at the last minute I had jumped into a clock, a grandfather clock like they've got downstairs, and I couldn't get out again, not for the moment, 'cause they had a Doberman. Do you know what a Doberman is?

PEARL:

Don't be so smart. Of course I know what a Doberman is.

POINT:

Good. So the Doberman sits in front of the clock and waits. I'm sitting inside and I fall asleep. Suddenly it strikes twelve.

PEARL:

Midnight.

POINT:

Exactly. Well, I'm not superstitious, but believe me, I was good and scared. When I got over my fright, I was so mad I ate up all the minutes and seconds, every last one of them. After that the clock wouldn't run.

PEARL:

Pish! How perfectly absurd! Tell me about the convent.

POINT:

You know that one already.

PEARL:

Who cares? Go on. Get started.

POINT:

Well, that was after my second trip to Paris. I went to a kind of lodginghouse.

PEARL:

An old people's home, you mean?

POINT:

That's right. A Catholic institution in Düsseldorf on the

Ratherbroich. Fine location. Right near the railroad
tracks, two steps from the junkyard, and the place itself,
believe you me, it was tops. Great big cellars, nice and
dark, plenty of cracks and dampness. I was rolling in
clover, hm, so to speak.

PEARL:

I can imagine. You always were a voluptuary. But what
about the nuns?

POINT:

Just what you'd expect. The kitchen and living quarters
were upstairs. And sometimes they came down to the
cellar to get something. I'd be on the lookout, and when
one of them came waddling in, I'd take quick aim and
dart in under her habit.

PEARL:

You're a riot.

POINT:

Then I'd climb up her leg, they wear heavy woolen stockings, and I'd give her a good nip in the calf, and she'd let
out a scream and drop everything.

PEARL:

What did she drop?

POINT:

Maybe a bowl. One time a dish full of peas. Full to the
brim. Believe you me. Soon as the nun was gone, I made
a beeline for the peas.

PEARL:

Stop, I'm getting weak.

POINT:

One time. Listen, one time, she dropped a pâté. D'you
know what that is?

PEARL:

No, I must admit I don't.

POINT:

You wouldn't. You haven't been in Paris.

PEARL:

Tell me what the nuns look like.

POINT:

What should they look like? Brown and fat, like baked potatoes. There was only one that looked different. Her name was Sister Alphonse Maria.

PEARL:

How come Alphonse Maria?

POINT:

That's the way it is sometimes with nuns. I don't know why myself.

PEARL:

And what did she look like?

POINT:

Come off it, you know all that. I've told you ten times.

PEARL:

But if it interests me? Just go on. Was your Alphonse Maria good-looking?

POINT:

Good-looking? Up top she was beautiful. But down below! D'you know what she had? She had freckles on her legs. All the way up.

PEARL:

How do you know?

POINT:

I saw it with my own eyes.

PEARL:

Where?

POINT:

In the cellar, of course, where else! She used to come down now and then and lock the door from inside, always real careful. Then she'd lift up her skirts whish-whish, take down her woolen stockings, and look at her legs. She'd stand there a good ten minutes. And look. And look.

PEARL:

They couldn't have been that bad.

POINT:

That's what you think. They were as white as maggots. All the way from the ankles to the Arc de Triomphe. And all covered with freckles.

PEARL:

What was her name again?

POINT:

Alphonse Maria, Sister Alphonse Maria.

PEARL:

What nonsense!

POINT:

Later the priests came down with some pasty-faced choir-boys and filled the whole place with incense and holy water. It was a shame.

PEARL:

What did they do that for?

POINT:

That's a dumb question! On account of me, naturally. They thought it was some kind of demon whishing under the nun's habit.

PEARL:

Pish! A fine demon you'd be.

POINT:

It's all very well for you to laugh, but I caught some of their lukewarm holy water. It didn't do me one bit of good, I assure you. It gave me bad dreams. Bad dreams. That was enough for me. I cleared out.

PEARL:

What about the nun with the freckles?

POINT:

Oh, they transferred her someplace. God only knows what she'd done, but you sometimes hear some pretty spicy stories about convents.

PEARL:

Yes, maybe so—Say, I'm hungry. What about you?

POINT:

Me. Oh no, not at all.

PEARL:

That's funny. How come?

POINT:

I'll never be hungry again.

PEARL:

What's that? You'll never be hungry again?

POINT:

That's right.

PEARL:

See here, you're not going to stand there and tell me with a straight face . . .

POINT:

Oh yes I am.

PEARL:

So you're not hungry?

POINT:

That's what I said. When I disappeared a while ago, I shat out my hunger. From now on the spirit will feed me. See?

PEARL:

No, I don't see at all. No self-respecting rat has any truck with the spirit.

POINT:

You musn't talk like that. The spirit makes you cool and transparent. In short, it makes you immortal. I'll outlive them all. The whole lot of them—even the cats.

(*The roof slowly darkens. The light goes on in the room.* NOAH *stands staring at the ceiling. The others all sitting or reclining*)

NOAH:

Somebody really ought to go up on the roof and chase those rats away. Henry?

HENRY:

Me? Why me?

NOAH:

I see. It's always the same. I'll have to do it myself.

LEO:

Let them live, Pop. They're on their last legs, just like us.

NOAH:

Be sensible. We've really got to get those rats off the roof.

YETTA:

You want them down here with us?

BETTY:

Oh no! Goodness, not that!

NOAH:

Don't be silly. We'll just sweep them into the water. (*He starts for the stairs.* LEO *holds him back by the coattails*)

LEO:

You stay right here. Didn't I tell you to leave those rats alone?

NOAH:

Why? Why are you suddenly so softhearted? They're not people.

LEO:

Rats are people, too. And that's that. (NOAH *sits down again among his inkwells*)

YETTA:

Don't bother with him, Leo. Tell us a story.

LEO:

I haven't got any story. What are you so busy about, Auntie?

BETTY:

Why, Leo, you know, I've told you. One, two, three, four, five, six little parasols. One for each of us.

LEO:

Don't bother making one for me. I'm going to the North Pole.

BETTY:

Never mind. Someday you'll be needing a parasol too.

LEO:

You're always worried about my welfare. Nix. I don't like it.

BETTY:

Oh well, now that my sister, your dear mother, is gone . . .

LEO:

Mamma didn't make parasols. She was always lying in bed, looking pale and offended.

BETTY:

She was never very well. You should try to remember that.

LEO:

No wonder, in this joint, with that inkwell nut.

BETTY:

Leo!

LEO:

Okay, okay. I know. She had cancer and the inkwells weren't to blame. Forget it.

NOAH:

You didn't even shed a tear at her funeral.

LEO:

What was there to cry about? You yourself said that people who die of cancer always go to heaven. Or didn't you?

YETTA:

Stop it. I'm sick of it. I've got it up to here. (*She goes to the window*) Look at those beds floating by. Empty, vacated beds. I wish I could be a bed like that, empty, tossing about. Not standing on four legs, under an idiotic oil painting, tied to the chamber pot and the bedside table, false teeth in glass of water, detective story with bookmark, dreaming the murder to the bitter end, and putting up with the seventy years that some people spend on earth from sheer habit. Maybe I'd drift into the woods, but first I'd shake off the pillow. If I were free, I'd say: Come! and then a cat, which would have drowned if I hadn't come along, would jump into my arms and be happy. Leo, for God's sake say something, or your friend. (YETTA *turns back to the room*) Oh go ahead, tell us something.

LEO:

Ain't nothing to tell.

HENRY:

Please tell us a story.

LEO (*with a severe look at* HENRY):

Shut up, hairdresser. Let Congo tell us something. He's a better liar.

YETTA:

I don't care who, as long as it's somebody. Otherwise the rain talks. And I know that story.

LEO:

Is Auntie sleeping?

YETTA:

I think so. And the old man too.

LEO:

Okay. It doesn't matter when or where. I was sitting in the circus.

CONGO:

It was in Saigon.

LEO:

Doesn't matter where, I said. In a circus, round like all circuses. Same smell too. Above me in the spotlight, in mid-air, the legs of a lady with a tinsel smile. (HENRY *laughs*) Say, I'm going to give your hairdresser a poke in the jaw.

YETTA:

What's that got to do with me?

LEO:

Okay. I will proceed. So this little lady had legs. They were made of porcelain. Damn it, I am still willing to certify that they were made of the purest porcelain.

CONGO:

We believe you.

YETTA:

Who cares what they were made of?

LEO:

I do. They were cool. As she swung—the lady was on a trapeze, you see—they got cooler and cooler. In the end they were ice. Two columns of ice leading to that little temple in the Arctic. Her North Pole—was inaccessible. No explorer who ever lived could have made it. Do you realize what that means? Ice up above you, high, but not so very high, halfway up the tent—and then way up in the big top. Ice! But delicate, charming, agile. Not ice in cones to lick, or ice in cubes, out of the refrigerator.

CONGO:

I see what you mean. Ice with joints. Makes you sweat to look at it.

LEO:

That's it. And then, what happened then? Snap, crackle, pop. The people began to clap. Made the whole thing silly. An avalanche of firecrackers! Haze, south wind, thaw.

YETTA:

And your lady?

LEO:

She flowed down the rope, she bent, she cracked, she dripped. She was dirty and slippery, her skin was dry, and

C

she was about thirty. Her smile was a puddle—as if some
horse had pissed.

CONGO:

What could you expect with all that applause?

YETTA:

Applause is always bad.

LEO:

I went to see her often.

CONGO:

But you knew what was going to happen.

LEO:

That's right. But I wanted to see her fall. I wondered
how it would be. Something like this. (*He drops a crystal
bowl.* NOAH *and* BETTY *start up*)

NOAH:

What happened?

YETTA:

Nothing. Go back to sleep.

NOAH:

Was that necessary?

LEO:

Yes, it was necessary. Do you understand? That sound.
That crash. The North Pole scattered all over the place.
From the Niger to the Arctic. But no applause. (NOAH
and BETTY *fall asleep again*)

YETTA:

And then?

LEO:

I waited for it every night.

YETTA:

And what happened?

LEO:

Nothing, of course. Once Pello came over to me.

CONGO:

Pello?

LEO:

Yeah. He was the clown.

YETTA:

What did he have to do with it?

LEO:

It's no use, he said. You'll have to shoot her down yourself. Well, I didn't exactly want to do that.—Look here,
Congo, why do you keep asking stupid questions? You
know the whole story by heart, and you know it's not true.

CONGO:

I know.

LEO:

So?

CONGO:

You tell it different every time; it's interesting. I'm the
only one that knows what really happened. You've forgotten.

LEO (*jumps up, sits down again*):

I want to go to the Arctic.

CONGO:

Okay, good. We'll go to the Arctic.

YETTA:

It's still raining right now. (*She stands up lazily*) You
think you're so smart, always talking about tomorrow.
Today it's raining. Today, that's something I know. You
know what today is? It's all this water. Get the bread
knife; cut yourself a slice if you feel like it. Today is you
people sitting there thinking. Think, think, think. You
look at this sweaterful of mine, and you think. But what
will it be like in twenty years? Christ, you can't just sit
there looking on while a pair of tits get longer and longer
and longer, until in the end they don't mean a thing. You,
that's what today is. You, my sweet little fiancé, you, the
old fool that's my father. And my dear aunt. She never
has enough. Always wants to look at a few more snap-
shots. If somebody came in with a blank little square and

said: "Look here, Auntie, this is God; just imagine, they've found a way to take his picture." You know what she'd say? "Gracious me, God! Why, that's exactly how I imagined him." And she'd paste him up in the album in between Uncle Stanislas and Cousin Bridget. That's what she'd do.

HENRY:

You are only expressing a passing state of mind.

YETTA:

Shut your trap! (*At the window*) Look at those beds out there. That would be something. Where they're going, nobody takes any pictures.

HENRY:

But there is a future. You've got to admit there's a future.

YETTA:

You're just a kid. Future. It's like a flight of stairs. There's always a floor above you and then another floor and then comes the roof, and then back down, one flight, two flights, to the cellar. You call that a future?

HENRY:

Can't you try to understand? You know perfectly well that the rain will stop and the sun will come out. I see it. O sun in radiant white raiment! I can see you raising your arm. On the inside it's fairest white, but on the back it's sunburned!

CONGO:

Looks like I'm going to have to give the choirboy the air. I don't care for Latin, and there's plenty of room on the roof.

YETTA:

Good idea. I'm fed up, too.

HENRY:

What have you got against me? You're just tormenting yourself. All this talk about ice and the Arctic. I can't stand it.

LEO:

Hm, I'm beginning to think . . .

HENRY:

I was in Florence once. I was crossing a square. I was wearing a summer suit. There was light everywhere and I had a feeling that there was sun inside me, in my head.

YETTA:

Now he's got sunstroke.

HENRY (*with mounting enthusiasm*):

I crossed the square, there was a flight of stairs, pigeons, pigeons everywhere, the stairs were covered with mother-of-pearl, it came from the pigeons, I picked up some, it brings luck . . .

LEO:

Congo?

HENRY:

And freedom and happiness. Happiness . . .

LEO:

Congo?

HENRY:

You don't even know what happiness is.

CONGO:

You're damn right about that, boy. (*He goes slowly toward* HENRY)

HENRY:

And you don't know what freedom is either.

CONGO:

Come along, sonny boy. You take a little turn on the roof now. Plenty of freedom up there. I think there's somebody there already. They'll be glad to hear you preach. They like that kind of thing. (*He takes hold of* HENRY *and pushes him up the stairs to the roof*)

HENRY:

No, no, no. Please. It's dark up there. You can't put me

out . . . it's getting dark . . . Night . . . (CONGO *closes the trap door*)

YETTA:

I don't know what's got into him. He's not usually that way. Sometimes he can be real nice.

LEO:

Congo?

CONGO:

What?

LEO:

Listen. I think we'll take a ship to Liverpool, and then . . .

YETTA:

Stop it! Stop it!

CONGO:

That's right, Leo. Calm down. We're going to stay here a little while. And besides—believe it or not—your sister appeals to me. (*He approaches* YETTA. *The room darkens. Light on the roof.* HENRY *is standing beside the chimney*)

POINT:

Hey, Pearl. Somebody's come up.

PEARL:

It's possible. But not one of our people.

POINT:

All I can say is that when this is over and we can come down, we're going to get out of here. I don't care where we go.

PEARL:

Better wait, my dear. We can always emigrate.

POINT:

You think there really are no sparrows here?

PEARL:

I thought you weren't hungry any more.

POINT:

Don't rub it in. He's coming this way.

(HENRY, *beside the chimney, moves; the rats in half darkness*)

HENRY:

Now she'll be thinking I'm angry with her. Actually I've forgiven her already. After a while they'll come and get me, and she'll say: Henry, let's make up, don't look so offended, I didn't mean what I said, come on down. That's the way she talks. And then she'll say even more: Come on—she'll say—tell us something, tell us about your silly sun if you feel like it. Leo has sold us his ice, now we are transparent and fragile. Of course I'll go down, sure, but I won't say a word. Silence comes easy to me. First let her stop fooling around with Congo. I wish I knew what she sees in him. Is it my fault that I'm so young? (*He sits down dejectedly*)

(*The rats in the light*)

PEARL:

Say, he's a philosopher.

POINT:

I think so, too. Well, then he won't hurt us.

PEARL:

Think so? I've heard that some philosophers can be downright mean.

POINT:

Oh yes, in writing. But in the rain, the ink runs and the driest philosopher is helpless. Once they get wet, all they believe in is wetness.

PEARL:

Look. He's thinking again.

(*The rats in the darkness.* HENRY *in the light*)

HENRY:

We were going to be married when I finished school. If my parents come to the wedding, that will make an impression on her. Especially my mother, she's still a fine figure of a woman. (HENRY *stares into the darkness, the rats in the light*)

POINT:

Say, he's no philosopher.

PEARL:

No, I guess not.

POINT:

Those people seem to have thrown him out.

PEARL:

I wonder why. I think he's sweet. So sensitive. So affectionate.

POINT:

I bet he's an only child.

PEARL:

Yes, he does seem rather spoiled.

POINT:

Maybe he was talking too much. Or maybe he was just one too many.

PEARL:

He's attractive, if you ask me. A little too milk-faced, but otherwise . . .

POINT:

Maybe they'll come and get him after a while.

PEARL:

Or maybe they'll all come up. They'll have to, pretty soon.

(Dark on the roof. In the room the area around the bed is lighted. On the bed lie CONGO *and* YETTA. LEO *is sitting on a footstool, his back to the bed, deep in thought. To the left in the half darkness,* AUNT BETTY *is sewing.* NOAH *is sorting inkwells)*

CONGO *(half singing)*:

It's raining, it's raining. The earth is getting wet.

YETTA:

Do you like to sing?

CONGO:

Kind of.

YETTA:

I used to like to sing.

CONGO:

Not any more?

YETTA:

Oh yes, but not as much I used to.

CONGO:

That's too bad.

YETTA:

Why?

CONGO:

Well, you could have sung something.

YETTA:

What? Now?

CONGO:

Why not? Do you know a song?

YETTA:

The Rain Song?

CONGO:

Is it sad?

YETTA:

I'm not sure.

CONGO:

It doesn't matter. If it makes me cry, I'll tell you to stop.

YETTA:

You, cry!

CONGO:

Why not?

YETTA:

Okay. (*Half singing, half speaking*)

The bird stands in the garden,
The leaf flies away to the north.
But I didn't write on it, I didn't write on it—

Because the rain can't read.
The little children cough,
And the big children die.
But I'm alive and kicking, I'm alive and kicking—
Because the rain has plans for me.

CONGO:

Because the rain has plans for you . . .

YETTA:

Do you like it?

CONGO:

Go on. There must be some more.

YETTA:

All right, if you want me to. (*She sings*)

Beetles have six legs,
I've got only two.
But here I stay, but here I stay—
'Cause it's raining everywhere the same.
The professor counts the stars.
The old folks count the years.
But I've stopped counting—I've stopped counting,
'Cause the rain forgot my birthday.

Want me to stop?

CONGO:

Isn't there any more?

YETTA:

Yes, I guess there is, but I thought . . .

CONGO:

Go on and sing. It's real nice.

YETTA:

I don't mind. (*Sings*)

The snail came much too late,
Love came much too soon.
But I didn't have to wait, I didn't have to wait—
Because the rain is always on time.

The sand wears cloaks of silk,
The snow puts on black velvet.
But I'm completely naked, I'm completely naked,
'Cause the rain is wearing my clothes.

(*Silence*)

CONGO:

Is that all?

YETTA:

No!

Hindenburg is dead,
And Adolf Hitler's gone.
And I'm dead too, and I'm dead too—
'Cause the rain's a coffin lid.

CONGO:

What's this stuff about coffin lids? Hindenburg, Hitler, good riddance. But a kid like you? With a build like that! How can you sing such stuff?

YETTA:

You wanted me to.

CONGO:

Was that the end?

YETTA:

No. I don't think so.

CONGO:

What do you mean, think? Is it going to be the end now?

YETTA:

Not yet—it never stops, not this song.

LEO (*sits up*):

I know the end.

CONGO:

You? Who ever said you could sing?

LEO:

I've been singing the whole time. You just weren't listening.

CONGO:

Well, go ahead.

LEO (*stands up*):

> Today is Tuesday morning,
> Tomorrow is yesterday night.
> No, I'm not gloomy, no, I'm not gloomy—
> 'Cause the rain is just a lousy joke.

Okay, all together now!

CONGO, LEO, *and* YETTA:

> 'Cause the rain is just a lousy joke!

CONGO:

Oh boy, oh boy. That was good. (LEO *turns away again*)

YETTA:

I hadn't ought to have sung.

CONGO:

Why not? It was real nice. It's cozy here, isn't it?

YETTA:

Yes, of course.

CONGO:

We get along fine, don't we? The two of us?

YETTA:

Sure.

CONGO (*sits up*):

What do you see in that guy? (*He points up toward the roof*)

YETTA:

Hell, you know how it is. He's not a bad kid.

CONGO:

Just kind of nuts.

YETTA:

Yes, sometimes. Maybe because he's so young.

CONGO:

That's possible. Planning to get married?

YETTA:

I don't know. Now that you're here.

CONGO (*surprised*):

I wouldn't want to interfere.

YETTA:

Natch. You'll be taking off when it stops raining.

CONGO:

Leo's got ants in his pants.

YETTA:

He wants to go to the North Pole. And then some other place.

CONGO:

That's right.

YETTA:

Too bad.

CONGO:

Yes, it's too damn bad. We get along so good. Don't we? (*He hugs her, laughing*)

YETTA:

Don't laugh.

CONGO:

Why not, kid? You laugh too. We'll be coming back.

YETTA:

Don't talk like that. You're still here, aren't you? Tell me something about yourself. You used to be a boxer?

CONGO:

I'll say.

YETTA:

Did you box when you were a kid?

CONGO:

I'll say. But forget it.

YETTA:

Tell me about it—Bruno!

CONGO:

All of a sudden, when I was about fifteen or sixteen, I'd had it. Damned if I know why. The guys in the club said: Stick it out, Bruno—at that time they were still calling me Bruno. Stick it out, they said. Just a few more rounds to go. You gotta stay. And I did. Desperation, I guess.

YETTA:

But you were good?

CONGO:

Sure, sure. Yes, I was good. (*He stares into space*)

YETTA:

But it's nice here too, isn't it?

CONGO:

Yes, sure.

YETTA:

You really think so?

CONGO:

Yes, damn it, of course. You got me all worn out.

YETTA (*laughing*):

That's the sweetest thing you ever said.

CONGO:

Where did you learn to . . .

YETTA:

Aw, cut it out.

CONGO:

From him (*pointing toward the roof*) or just around?

YETTA:

Bruno, please.

CONGO:

All right, all right. I didn't mean any harm.

YETTA:

Now I can hear the rain again.

CONGO:

How was that again with the beetle?

YETTA:

> The beetle has six legs,
> I've got only two. (*Sings*)
> But here I stay, but here I stay—
> 'Cause it's raining everywhere the same.

YETTA *and* CONGO:

> 'Cause it's raining everywhere the same.

YETTA:

As long as it rains, you'll stay with me. And when it rains again for a long long time, you'll come back.

CONGO:

That's just about it. But don't worry if it don't rain for a while.

LEO (*slowly sitting up*):

Well, Congo, how you getting on with my little sister?

YETTA:

What is it to you?

LEO:

Don't be so touchy. Excuse the interruption, but my feet have been trying to tell me something. I can't be sure from up here, but I've got a hunch that it's going to be kind of damp around here . . . What do you say we go up and see how your boy friend's getting along? He must be kind of bored.

CONGO (*reaches down to the floor*):

His feet are right. It's coming through. Don't worry, kid. We'll take some things. A couple of blankets is all we need. And maybe Aunt Betty has . . . Hey, Aunt Betty!

BETTY (*wakes up*):

Goodness, I must have dozed off. I had a dream. I don't remember what. No, I really don't remember. Did somebody call?

CONGO:

I took the liberty. Is one of your parasols ready?

BETTY:

Oh, yes, of course. Here it is. How do you like it? (*She exhibits a parasol*)

CONGO:

It's marvelous. Give it here. The parasol will be put to its proper use.

BETTY:

But the sun isn't out.

CONGO:

That don't matter. The rain is. (*He jumps up*) Better step on it! (*Takes the parasol and some blankets*) You come too, Auntie. We're sick of it down here. We need a change of air. Altitude!

BETTY:

Gracious! Water! Noah!

NOAH:

Well, my dear, it looks as if we'll have to sit on the stairs.

CONGO:

Let's get going. We wouldn't want to catch cold. (*To* LEO) Here, hold this.

YETTA:

You're going to carry me?

CONGO:

I'll carry you. As long as it rains. I'll carry you. (LEO, CONGO, *and* YETTA *climb up on the roof.* NOAH *and* AUNT BETTY *make their way over tables and benches to the stairs*)

NOAH:

Go, go! Good riddance. What have you made of my house? You have filled it with shame, with filth higher than the water . . . and the water's rising . . .

BETTY:

Why are you so nasty-minded?—They've been so quiet.

NOAH:

Just wait! The water will catch up with you. Go on, climb

the stairs. Do you think water can't climb stairs? The water will follow you like a postman. It will catch up with you on the roof, and it won't be bringing you good news. Not on your tintype. Look here, Betty, I've brought this along. We'll keep it with us. (*He opens a black book and reads*) "The same day were all the fountains of the deep broken up, and the windows of heaven were opened."

(*The stage slowly darkens*)

Act II

(The same scene. The roof lighted. HENRY *and* LEO *to the right and left of the chimney. At the left edge of the roof, the rats. At the right edge, under the parasol,* CONGO *and* YETTA *wrapped in blankets)*

PEARL *(whispering)*:

At first I thought they were going to hurt us.

POINT:

They don't even see us; they're looking at something else.

PEARL:

Something else is good. There's nothing to see. Do you call that a landscape?

POINT:

That's not what I meant. It's themselves they see, and that's enough for them.

PEARL:

I should think so. When I look at myself, I have a feeling that the rain has made holes in me.

POINT:

Don't worry, old girl. You still look good to me. Besides, the rain is beginning to let up. Once this thing is over, you'll have a good feed, and then I'll polish you up bright.

PEARL:

Oh, oh! Heavens alive!

POINT:

What's wrong?

PEARL:

Oh, what a fright I had! I'm sitting here looking. There's something white hanging in the tree over there. So I see

this white thing and I must have been dreaming a little.
It begins to move, it turns into a figure, and guess what
it is?

POINT:

A medical corps major.

PEARL:

Exactly. And he's got a syringe in his hand and he keeps
saying: Well, my sweet little guinea pig, we're going to do
an interesting little experiment. And he comes closer and
closer.

POINT:

You mustn't think about those things, my dear.

PEARL (*crying*):

My whole family!

POINT:

Yes, I know. When this thing has stopped and the roads
are clear, we'll get up a little pilgrimage. A lot of the folks
will come. It will do you good.

PEARL:

Where will we go?

POINT:

To Hamelin of course. To Hamelin.

(*The light shifts to the chimney*)

HENRY:

What made you come up here?

LEO (*surprised*):

What! He's still around?

HENRY:

What have you come for?

LEO:

I thought he had dissolved long ago.

HENRY:

Why did . . .

LEO:

Shut up, hairdresser. We're here, period.

HENRY:

But why?

LEO:

Will you shut up! How do I know? Curiosity, boredom, homesickness—all the same thing. Now are you satisfied?

HENRY:

But your sister. I love her.

LEO:

Then everything's perfect.

HENRY:

You fellows just come along and take whatever you like.

LEO:

That's right. But you're a hairdresser. You'll never understand.

YETTA (*sits up*):

Quit it. (*Softly*) Pipe down.

LEO:

He started it, kid. This sugar-plum of yours always has to open his yap and ask questions.—Congo!

YETTA:

Aw, be still. He's sleeping.

LEO:

Who cares?

YETTA:

Leave him alone, Leo. It won't be long.

LEO:

That's just it. We've got to get ready. We'll be leaving soon. Congo!

CONGO (*wakes up*):

What's up? Time to be going? (*He holds his hand out in the rain*) It's still raining.

LEO:

Not much. We'll be getting out of here soon. We'll take the boat to Liverpool. Do you hear me?

CONGO:

Every word. You said Liverpool. I'll attend to everything. But first I have a few little things to tell your sister. (*He wraps himself in the blanket with* YETTA)

LEO:

Did you see that, son? That's the way my best friend treats me.

HENRY:

Why don't you make him stop? (*Pointing to Congo*)

LEO:

Why?

HENRY:

She's your sister after all.

LEO:

My sister, maybe she is. But get this, son, everything that's happened here, it's all for your own good. You're meaning to get married later on, aren't you?

HENRY:

I don't need him for that.

LEO:

Take it easy. Take it easy. I've been told that it's not so simple. A young kid like you, a little hairdresser at that . . . my sister expects . . .

HENRY:

I'm as good a man as he is.—You fellows drag everything in the mud.

LEO:

It's the only thing to do. Treasures have to be hidden. Gold is so shiny, it attracts too much attention. Spread a little muck over it, and nobody'll see it. You can always polish it up later on.

HENRY:

Nobody will ever be able to polish *that* clean again.

LEO:

I hope you are not trying to insinuate that my sister isn't the genuine article, pure twenty-four-carat gold. If that's what you're trying to say, I'll beat the . . . (*He draws back his fist*) Good! That's better. Don't keep looking over there. You were taught good manners, I'm willing to bet you come of a very good family. What does your father do anyway?

HENRY:

He's a doctor.

LEO:

Not bad. That's something to live up to. Stop looking. Be a gentleman. And now listen to me, I'm going to tell you a story.

HENRY:

I don't want to listen.

LEO:

What, you don't want to listen! Your father's a doctor and you won't listen to a story. Better listen, kid, it's instructive, especially for you. I knew a man once down there, he was well heeled. He had a very special way of handling women, and that's what I was getting at. Not that he was so very polite. Far from it. He had a kind of a trestle put up in his back yard, and every Sunday afternoon—he only did it on Sunday afternoon—he used to take a couple of pounds of soft soap and a bundle of old newspapers. And do you know what he did then? (LEO's *story fades into whispers. The light moves to the rats*)

PEARL:

Say, Point! He's whispering. Do you think he's talking about me? They won't stop at anything when they're hungry.

POINT:

You're always taking such a dark view of things.

PEARL:

It wouldn't be the first time. In 1871 in Paris . . .

POINT:

Oh, in those days. Besides, it was Frenchmen. Such things don't happen any more.

PEARL:

You never can tell. When they get to a certain stage, it doesn't matter if they're Frenchmen or Eskimos, they stop at nothing. I'm scared.

POINT:

Nonsense.

PEARL:

Well, just the same, I'm scared.

POINT:

What about? It's all over. What can happen now?

PEARL:

I wonder if they're scared too.

POINT:

I doubt it. That's too much of an effort for them. They only get scared in the movies, because then they're comfortably seated and it's dark and they've paid their money. Besides, they know the picture won't last more than an hour or two. Under such conditions they can afford to be a little scared and nibble chocolate.

PEARL:

But this flood?

POINT:

They don't even notice. They're only thinking of what they'll do when it subsides and the streetcar is running again.

PEARL:

I guess humans are pretty tough.

POINT:

Yes, Pearl, almost as tough as rats.

(*The roof darkens, a dim light goes on in the room.* BETTY *and* NOAH *huddled on a crate under a blanket*)

NOAH:

It's a good thing I made the catalogue so small. It's complete, it's clear, but it's not too bulky to move.

BETTY:

And remember how I used to scold you. I was always saying: Don't write so small, Noah, you'll ruin your eyes.

NOAH:

I'm sure you meant well, but you will never know how mistaken you were. I've got everything right here.

BETTY:

I'm so glad for you, Noah; I only wish I had been so far-sighted. The photographs are falling apart. The dampness . . .

NOAH:

Silly goose. The damage is insignificant, negligible. It can easily be mended. Besides, the water has stopped rising. At last we can breathe easy. It was almost at our necks, and now it's sliding off again without saying why.

BETTY:

We'll soon be able to stretch our legs. I wonder what the children are doing.

NOAH:

The children? They're not our children any more. Didn't they go away, didn't they leave us flat?

BETTY:

How can you say such things! We were free to . . .

NOAH:

Go up on the roof with them, is that what you mean, and let everything go to rack and ruin down here?

BETTY:

We could have taken a few things with us.

NOAH:

No, no, no. I'd never have done that.

BETTY:

Oh, Noah, you're so stiff-necked.

NOAH:

So proud, you mean. Well, yes.

BETTY:

Proud or stiff-necked, it's all the same. My policy is to stay young with the young folks. I would have gone. They are so fresh and unspoiled. I do like the young folks.

NOAH:

Nobody held you back. You could have gone. You can still go.

BETTY:

Nonsense. An old woman like me. No, I don't know. You or somebody else, something held me back. But what difference does it make? The water's falling.

(*The room darkens. The roof is lighted*)

LEO:

I almost think the rain has stopped.

CONGO:

It stopped long ago.

LEO:

It was high time. You could have said something. Some friend you turned out to be.

YETTA:

Maybe it will start again.

HENRY:

Oh, no!

YETTA:

What do you know about it?

HENRY:

Something has happened. Something has torn . . .

YETTA:

Cut it out!

LEO:

Leave him alone. Say your piece, sonny boy.

HENRY:

Yes, really, something has torn. I heard it. That whole gray curtain is rotting. In a minute it will disintegrate and set something free.

YETTA:

Oh, you and your God-damned sun!

HENRY:

Exactly. And it will point at you and you and you—and say: So that's what you look like, gray, gray inside and gray outside.

LEO:

Right you are, little sister. He's still a hairdresser. How could you get mixed up with this weather prophet?

YETTA:

What else was there for me to do?

CONGO:

Why is everybody looking so glum? Aren't we almost dry? Where's that bottle? (*He pulls out a bottle*)

LEO:

Let's drink to the end of the rainy season and the beginning of the Ice Age.

YETTA:

There you go starting up again.

LEO:

But baby, that's the way life is. Mustn't let it get you down. First a little rain, and then we go skating, and then . . .

CONGO:

First let's have a drink.

LEO:

Sure. The skating will keep.

(LEO, CONGO, *and* YETTA *sit together.* YETTA *with the bottle*)

YETTA:

Let's drink. Let's pretend it's still raining and the rain is flowing into us and slowly rising. (*She drinks*)

CONGO (*to* HENRY):

Don't stand there looking glum. Have a drink.

HENRY:

No.

CONGO:

Don't take on, kid. You'll get her back.

HENRY:

I don't want a drink.

YETTA:

Leave him alone, Bruno, if he doesn't feel like it.

(*The sun bursts through the clouds, a rainbow in the background*)

PEARL:

What did I tell you? The sun's coming out.

POINT:

It was bound to.

PEARL:

Oh—and the rainbow. It looks . . . it looks . . . gorgeous.

POINT:

That's just the way I like 'em. Kind of moldy, makes you want to nibble at it.

PEARL:

If only we could.

POINT:

What do those colors remind me of? Those colors. Those colors! For two cents I'd take up anthroposophy.

PEARL:

Nibbling would be better. Just imagine. Just us two. You start on the left and me on the right.

POINT:

Get ready, get set, and at go we go.

PEARL:

And meet in the middle.

POINT:

And down we go.

PEARL:

No, silly. We leave one stripe, the yellow one.

POINT:

Looks too greasy for me anyway.

PEARL:

Same here. And we slide down on it. It looks just right.
Ooh, I'm all pins and needles. What do you think of that
little shading, the way it merges . . . so gently . . . into
orange. It looks so sweet, so . . . oh, I don't know what
to say.

POINT:

Wouldn't it be wonderful!—Say, take a look at them.

PEARL:

Don't mention those people to me. They have no eye for
the wonders of nature. For those delicate tints and shad-
ings. When they can't think of anything else to do, they
start drinking.

POINT:

I think we ought to start . . .

PEARL:

You think we` . . .

POINT:

Yes, exactly. As I know my humans, they'll be getting
back to normal. Setting traps and that kind of thing.

PEARL:

Come to think of it, we haven't done so badly up here.
Why wouldn't we stay? As a symbol that things are picking up again?

POINT:

These people wouldn't understand. They haven't got it
in them. People nowadays have lost their feeling for true
symbols. If we were doves, genuine doves of peace . . .

PEARL:

My goodness, with a green sprig in our bills!

POINT:

And that loyal look.

PEARL:

We'd bill and coo.

POINT:

And artists would paint our pictures. And poets would write poems about us . . .

PEARL:

La Paloma, the white dove. They'd dance the tango to us.

POINT:

And we could show ourselves in the streets.

PEARL:

And hold up the traffic with never a fear.

POINT:

The cars would have to stop. A policeman would come.

PEARL:

But a friendly one.

POINT:

Of course. Policemen are always friendly with doves.

PEARL:

He'd go shoo-shoo-shoo . . .

POINT:

And smile and clap his lovely white gloves.

PEARL:

Oh, you sweet little doves of peace, would you kindly let the traffic pass?

POINT:

Just for two little minutes.

PEARL:

Yes, that's how it would be. We could eat out of their hands.

POINT:

Not bad.

PEARL:

Well, what do you say, are we staying or leaving? You promised to take me to Hamelin for the big annual family reunion and now . . .

POINT:

And so I will. I keep my promises. Then you agree that the time has come?

PEARL:

Of course. It will be simple. Over the wall and around the garden, we'll easily get to the railroad—amazing how quickly the water is falling. You look so thoughtful, Point. Is something wrong?

POINT:

No, not at all. Thoughts, memories—you know how it is.

PEARL:

All right, you can tell me.

POINT:

In my student days I was living in a library. One day—I was just eating the last chapter of a book—something very intelligent, very intellectual, on Bible paper if I'm not mistaken. No, I don't remember the title, it doesn't matter. But in those days I used to read at meals.

PEARL:

What did it say?

POINT:

It said: "The rats leave the sinking ship."

PEARL:

Hm.

POINT:

What do you say to that? Ship was meant symbolically, of course.

PEARL:

Yes, of course. A wise saying. Do you think they'll catch on? About the ship and the sinking?

POINT:

Maybe. Unless some dopey dove comes flying by with a weed in its bill.

PEARL:

Yes, maybe it will dawn on them that we've cleared out for very definite reasons.

POINT:

Once I read in the paper: The ship went down with man and mouse. Not a word about rats. (POINT *and* PEARL *disappear behind the chimney.* YETTA *stands up*)

LEO:

The rats are gone. It's going to be sad.

CONGO:

Is there anything we could do to make you sadder?

LEO:

Music affects me quickest.

YETTA:

We had music as long as the rats were here.

LEO:

And now it's intermission.

CONGO:

What kind of music do you want? Something special, an aria?

LEO:

It doesn't matter. Something gay for my money. Singing is sure-fire with me.

CONGO:

An aria then. Go on, Yetta. Your melancholy brother is in the mood for music.

YETTA:

Why doesn't he scratch himself?

CONGO:

Don't be like that. Sing something about our love. Or some kind of good-by.

YETTA:

Some heroes you turned out to be. When it's time to leave, they get sad, they get a belly-ache. A little tra-la-la, and their noble spirits rise again.

CONGO:

It's only because we're such music lovers. Would you like Congo to give you the keynote?

YETTA (*half speaking, half singing*):

On our way home
Over the long rainbow,
We were very tired.
We held on to the railing,
And we were afraid
It would fade away.

On my way home
Over the long rainbow,
I was very tired.
I clung to you and the railing.
I was afraid
That you and the rainbow both
Would fade away.

That's that. Are you satisfied? You can go now if you want to. In fact, beat it. The sooner the better.

CONGO (*gets up*):

Come along, Leo. She's right. You've been talking the whole time about leaving. So don't drag it out.

LEO:

Did I say anything about leaving?

CONGO:

It seems to me I heard something of the sort.

HENRY:

The whole time, ever since you've been here, you've been saying you wanted to leave.

LEO:

My oh my. The little door mat is feeling his oats. His time is coming, he says to himself. Okay, we'll leave him. (*He jumps up*) What should we take with us?

CONGO:

Nothing, son. We'll even leave the umbrella. I'll plant it on this pedestal. (*He stands the parasol up in the chimney*) Now it's a parasol again. We wouldn't want the sun to shine in on our dear friends through the chimney. That would be too sad.

YETTA:

You don't have to feel sorry for me. Just get out.

LEO:

I don't feel sorry for you, little sister. If I feel sorry for anybody, it's myself.

(LEO *in the lead, all four climb down the stairs.* NOAH *in the midst of terrible disorder.* BETTY *in the doorway leading to the devastated garden*)

BETTY:

Oh, Noah, it's so terrible.

NOAH:

Just as I expected. Everything buried in mud.

LEO:

Ah, here's the family. How goes it, Auntie? Where are your parasols?

BETTY:

Why, Leo, there you are again. Have you young folks been getting on nicely together?

CONGO:

Harmony reigns as far as the eye can see. The altitude has done us good.

BETTY:

That's just what I've been telling your father. You see, Noah, the young folks need to be by themselves.

D

LEO:

The parasols. I asked you where the parasols were.

BETTY:

Just a little patience, Leo. They'll be ready in half an hour. I've hung them out in the air, they were a little damp. Gracious, how the garden looks! (*She runs out into the garden*)

NOAH:

It's a good thing you've come. There's work to be done. Not just the collection. I've already sorted out some of it. Watch me, this is how it's done. Very carefully we loosen the labels—some have come loose all by themselves—then we paste them on a cardboard and try to decipher the old markings. I'm sure a good many of them can be made out, but even so, as I was saying, there will be lots of work. Every piece will have to be identified and relabeled. My idea is that we should modernize the card index. It needs to be simplified, though of course we had better keep the old regional arrangement.

CONGO:

Am I getting you straight? You want to start in right away?

NOAH:

Oh no. Of course not. The collection can wait a little while. First the garden. If the whole lot of us pitch in, we'll have it shipshape in no time. It's a funny thing, but you can't imagine how strong I feel, strong . . .

LEO:

You always were pretty strong.

NOAH:

That's a fact. But now it's different. We're starting all over from rock bottom. But this time we know what we're after. There's no time to lose. Maybe we can find some old clothes and rubber boots. I'll go first, but don't keep me waiting. Henry!

HENRY:

Yes, Daddy, right away. You'll come too, won't you, Yetta?

YETTA:

Sure. Go on. I told you I'd come, didn't I? (HENRY *follows* NOAH)

LEO:

Can you beat that! (*He kicks one of the crates*) All this shit! Can you imagine wanting to catalogue shit?

CONGO:

Forget it, Leo. As long as he collects inkwells, he won't collect ears. It's harmless. Don't give him any bad ideas.

LEO:

It's him that gives me bad ideas. If it weren't so boring and didn't provide the shock effect in every other play, I'd kill him. Parricide!

CONGO:

Yeah, don't touch it.

LEO:

But we gotta do something before we fade out. (*He looks around*) I've got it. The clock!

CONGO:

What about it? It's busted. It only looks like a clock.

LEO:

They'll have it repaired right away.

CONGO:

Might be. Why shouldn't they?

LEO:

We'll take it with us. Let's go. Pick it up.

CONGO:

What, the whole thing? I thought you were going to the North Pole. Get a load of that, Yetta. Me and Leo or Leo and me, the two of us at the North Pole, with this clock.

> At the North Pole stood a grandfather clock,
> It didn't tick, it didn't tock.

With frozen ears we stood and gazed,
No pulse, no breath. The eye seemed glazed.

LEO:

Sure, let's furnish the North Pole.

CONGO:

Do we really have to?

LEO:

You can see they don't need it around here.

CONGO:

But what will they do without the big hand and the little
hand, and all those indispensable minutes in between?

YETTA:

How long are you going to stand here arguing?

CONGO:

Yetta, my child. You must see my point. This nasty Leo
wants to take the clock with everything that's in it.

YETTA:

It's all one to me. Take it or leave it. So long as you clear
out.

LEO:

Pick it up, Congo.

CONGO:

Okay, but you take the front end.

LEO:

Not I. You're so strong. You used to be a boxer, remember . . .

YETTA:

Just blow . . .

CONGO:

See here, Yetta's getting angry. She agrees that you should
go first.

YETTA:

For all I care, you can saw it in two.

CONGO:

That's an idea, Leo, let's saw it in two.

LEO:

All right, so you won't take the front end. So I'll take it. Sawing is out of the question. Pick it up, I'll go first.

CONGO:

Okay. But I don't like it.

(*As they are about to pick up the clock, it opens and a man steps out. He has on a blue arm band with a white dove on it.*)

INSPECTOR:

Forgive the intrusion. But before you take this clock away, or before you wantonly reduce it in size and so destroy it, I shall be obliged to make an inventory of loss and damage. I am from the local Damage Inspection and Quick Relief Office. Whenever a catastrophe occurs, it is our duty to be on the spot immediately.

CONGO:

You're on the spot all right. But say, what's that thing on your arm band?

INSPECTOR:

A dove. After floods we always wear a dove. After fires, we wear the famous phoenix rising from the ashes. Are you one of the occupants of this house?

CONGO:

Well, I don't know exactly.

INSPECTOR:

Please answer with deliberation and precision. Are you a local resident?

YETTA:

No, they're just visiting. Only four persons live here. I'm one and the other three are in the garden.

INSPECTOR:

Then I shall enter four persons on my list. (*He takes a list from his briefcase*)

YETTA:

Yes, do that, exactly four. The other two are going to disappear in a very few minutes.

LEO:

Now see what you've done. With all your dawdling we are compelled to leave in undignified haste.

CONGO:

Let's take him along. The little man, I mean.

LEO:

Not a bad idea, but he'll need a new arm band for the polar regions, with something symbolic on it. The Snow Queen, maybe.

CONGO:

Too much bother. Better leave him.

LEO:

Besides, it could be embarrassing. Suppose the three of us are up there at the Pole and this goblin gets the idea of writing up our loss and damages. My loss is my own business.

(*They begin to tip the clock over*)

INSPECTOR:

Stop! What are you doing with that clock? Is it on the inventory? Have you the right to dispose of it? Have you a written authorization?

YETTA:

Don't get excited. It's our farewell present to them. If we had a piano, they could take that too. They're crazy about music.—So will you finally take the clock and clear out. I'll even open the door for you.

INSPECTOR:

I shall have to make a note of this removal.

YETTA:

Go ahead.—Leo.

LEO:

Now what?

YETTA:

Are you going to leave just like that?

LEO:

You want me to cry? Oh, you want me to say good-by. Good-by.

YETTA:

Till when?

LEO:

Till when? Till it rains again, a good solid rain. Then we'll come climbing out of some crate again. So good-by.

CONGO:

Just a minute. Do you know the story about the shoelace that cost eight times as much as the shoe? Hm. You don't? I'll tell you the story, Yetta. But not now. Next time. (CONGO *and* LEO *exit with the clock*)

YETTA:

Is that all? Do I have to stay here, thinking the whole time that our clock is standing at the North Pole and that some shoelace is more expensive than the shoe that goes with it?—Now what do you want?

INSPECTOR:

As I told you, Miss, I have to inspect the damage. But it won't be long. I take it that the damage is only partial. There has been no loss of human life, I trust?

YETTA:

No. We're all still alive. Now go away.

INSPECTOR:

Just one moment. Have you a wish? I mean, are you in need of something? And let me leave you one of our informative and comforting pamphlets: "Man and Disaster" it's called.

HENRY (*from the garden*):

Yetta, Yetta.

YETTA:

I'm coming.—You ask if I have a wish. Why not, if

you're in the business. I wish it would rain again and rain and keep raining until there's water up to here, up to here.

(Slowly she leaves the room)

CURTAIN

Onkel, Onkel

A Play in Four Acts

Translated by Ralph Manheim

Cast of Characters

BOLLIN, a systematizer

SPRAT, a thirteen-year-old girl

SLICK, a fourteen-year-old boy

SOPHIE, a girl of about sixteen

MRS. DOMKE, Sophie's mother

GREENSWARD, a forester

MIMI LANDELLA, a prima donna

BODO, a photographer

Act I

Prologue

(BOLLIN *is sitting on a park bench.* SLICK *and* SPRAT *on roller skates are circling around him. The children come close and stand looking at* BOLLIN)

SPRAT:

How about this guy?

SLICK:

Is he new?

SPRAT:

Naw, everybody knows him.

SLICK:

Then it's him?

SPRAT:

Of course. He draws boxes in the sand with a stick. All the same size. And then he crosses them off.

SLICK:

He ain't got much.

SPRAT:

Not even a father and mother.

SLICK:

D'you think he?

SPRAT:

Wanna bet?

SLICK:

Ask him.

SPRAT:

There's a button missing on his coat.

SLICK:

And he needs new shoelaces. He's a crummy number. Why should we bother with him? Okay if he had sumpin, but look at him.

SPRAT:

Hey, mister? You lonesome, mister?

SLICK:

Maybe he's got a toothache. Look, he's got a watch. Ask him if he's got sumpin for us. Any old thing.

SPRAT:

Mister, aintcha got sumpin for us?

SLICK:

Take a look.—Wanna bet he's got sumpin?

(BOLLIN *looks up and takes a bag of candy out of his pocket. He opens it ceremoniously and holds it out to the children*)

SPRAT:

Think it's real?

SLICK:

Cheap stuff.

SPRAT:

Ugh, it's sticky!

SLICK:

Better not take any, Sprat. It's only to look at.

SPRAT:

Did you make it yourself, mister?

SLICK:

Ask him if he ain't got sumpin else. How about his watch? Or his fountain pen?

SPRAT:

This here?

SLICK:

Or that there.

SPRAT:

D'you hear, mister? Sumpin else. A watch or a fountain pen.

SLICK:

Any old thing. It don't have to be new.

SPRAT:

Aintcha?

SLICK:

Give it here.

SPRAT:

You'll get it back.

SLICK:

But first you got to hand it over.

SPRAT *and* SLICK (*half singing*):

> Mister, mister, aintcha got a thing,
> Mister, just a little thing,
> Any little thing.
> Mister, mister, aintcha, aintcha,
> Aintcha, aintcha, aintcha got
> Any little dingus,
> Hidden in your pocket?

(BOLLIN *slowly stands up and holds out the bag of candy to the children. The children laugh and skate away backwards, still laughing.* BOLLIN *shakes his fist at them*)

BOLLIN:

They don't want my candy.—Nobody wants my candy. (*He takes a candy and sucks*) I'll teach them. I've drawn ten diagrams and it always works. A man's only got to be true to himself. I'll show them. And if they don't want candy, they'll get something else. (*He exits through the curtain*)

Influenza

(A sickroom; SOPHIE, *wearing glasses, is lying in bed with a muffler around her neck. She is holding a newspaper and working on the crossword puzzle. Beside the bed a chair and bedside table. On the table: medicines.—Under the bed:* BOLLIN, *visibly nervous)*

SOPHIE:

Thirty-four across, four letters. Precipitation. Rain or hail? It could be either. But thirty-nine: Cheese-producing region in Holland? I've got it. Limburg! L-i-m-b-u-r-g. Now twelve down, twelve letters? No, six across, a contagious disease, what a funny coincidence!

*(*BOLLIN *springs nimbly out from under the bed, takes a notebook from his coat pocket, hops about the room studying the situation, and takes a menacing stance by the bed.* SOPHIE *takes off her glasses and examines him calmly and attentively)*

BOLLIN:

First take inventory, and then . . . ? No closet, no curtain. Normally creaky floor. Ordinary window, shutters closed. Self-color wallpaper pattern, light switch, double plug, sixty-watt bulb. Pretty drab for a young girl's room. I wonder why. *(He writes)*

SOPHIE:

Ah! I've got twelve down! Pen-i-ten-tia-ry.

BOLLIN:

Is there anybody else around here?

SOPHIE:

You mustn't come so close to my bed.—Is indicated by a yellow flag, ten across.

BOLLIN:

Listen, young lady. I asked you if there was anybody else around here.

SOPHIE:

Nice people say good afternoon.

BOLLIN:

All right, good afternoon. And now will you kindly tell me who lives here: father, mother, grandma, sister?

SOPHIE:

My brother's on duty.

BOLLIN:

Noted. When does he get off?

SOPHIE:

I refuse to answer unless you step back at least three paces. You really ought to be more careful.

BOLLIN:

Nonsense. I need it for my statistics. I've got to know when your brother's due here.

SOPHIE:

Go back behind the chair at least. I insist. (BOLLIN *steps back*) That's better. So you've got to know when my brother comes home? What day is it? Wednesday?

BOLLIN:

Yesterday was Tuesday.

SOPHIE:

Then he'll probably be late. On Wednesday he has to stop at the precinct station after work and type service reports.

BOLLIN:

Precinct station? Service? I keep hearing words that sound like precinct and service. Is he in the forestry service? Is he a gamekeeper?

SOPHIE (*laughs*):

Addi? How could our Addi be a gamekeeper? But it fits. Forestry official, ten letters.—Why, Addi couldn't tell the difference between a wild boar and a toadstool. He's with the police.

(BOLLIN *jumps*)

BOLLIN:

Crime squad?

SOPHIE:

Goodness no! You must have seen him. He's always on
the corner of Weaver Street and Magdeburg Street. Go
and watch him when you have time. When Addi's on
duty, everything goes all right. Never an accident, not
even a traffic jam. And he's never cross.

BOLLIN (*with an embarrassed laugh*):

So he's only a traffic cop.

SOPHIE:

Only?

BOLLIN (*pulling himself together*):

Yes, only. And now let's get to the point. Age? Fourteen,
fourteen and a half? Have you begun to menstruate, and
if so, when?

SOPHIE:

I can't allow you to come so close. I'm almost sixteen,
believe it or not.—And I don't see any need to answer
the second question.

BOLLIN:

Hm. Right on the borderline. Well, in case of doubt I'd
better see for myself, examine the details. (*He pulls off her
blankets*)

SOPHIE:

I'm freezing.

BOLLIN:

There we are. Just within the limit. Her age might put
her beyond it, but the doll proves . . .

SOPHIE:

I'm really freezing. (BOLLIN *drops the blankets but keeps
the doll*)

BOLLIN:

. . . that in certain cases the doll age . . . Do you
always keep it in bed with you?

SOPHIE:

That's Pinky. She's called Pinky because she's all pink.
Please give me back my Pinky.

BOLLIN (*puts* PINKY *on the bedside table*):

But to be on the safe side I'd better check the over-all
picture by reviewing the facts.

SOPHIE:

I hope you didn't catch anything just now.

BOLLIN:

Sixteen years old. Pajamas, Pinky—Catch anything.

(BOLLIN *laughs. Loud at first, his laughter then becomes
more subdued*) That's a good one. Imagine Bollin getting
sick.

SOPHIE:

What was the name again? Bollin?

BOLLIN:

Imagine Bollin catching anything from a little brat.
Never heard of Bollin? Never seen the name? The man
who finally carried statistics to their logical conclusion.
That's Bollin. Uncompromisingly methodical. Bollin is
always logical.—Take off your pajamas. Well, what are
you waiting for?

SOPHIE:

Don't be unreasonable. I had a hundred and two this
morning.

BOLLIN:

Go on, sister. Peel. I'm not joking. I seldom joke.

SOPHIE:

Certainly not.

BOLLIN:

What! You defy me?

SOPHIE:

Please don't be angry, but when Dr. Cushman dropped
in this morning, he said . . .

BOLLIN:

Who cares what he said. Take them off. I want to be Pinky too.

SOPHIE:

But the doctor . . .

BOLLIN:

That's irrelevant.

SOPHIE:

Maybe for you, but not for me. You can't imagine how much school I've missed already. And it's only another five weeks to Easter.—Would you kindly hand me the glass?

BOLLIN:

Wrong. It's exactly six weeks.

SOPHIE:

That's true, to Easter Sunday. But they make up the report cards a week before. Do you think I'll make it? Of course my friend brings me my homework every day, but . . .

BOLLIN:

How old is she?

SOPHIE:

Ella is six months younger than I am, but she looks much older.

BOLLIN:

Hm. And when is Ella coming?—Make a note of that.

SOPHIE:

She comes every afternoon about six. But she's only allowed to put the lessons in the mailbox. Ella's mother is afraid . . .

BOLLIN:

More nonsense. Let her come in. What's she afraid of?

SOPHIE:

What a question! Because I've got the flu. When will

you get that through your head? And now, won't you
hand me the glass?

BOLLIN:

May I ask what's in it? (*Hands her the glass*)

SOPHIE:

Lemonade. (*Drinks*) Thank you, Mr. . . . What was the
name again?

BOLLIN (*notes*)

These details make me sad.—Bollin.

SOPHIE:

Thank you very much, Mr. Bollin. (*Drinks again*) I wish
I could offer you something, but unfortunately . . .

BOLLIN:

Don't put yourself out for me.—But to dispel any possible doubt, do you mind? (*He hands her a thermometer*)

SOPHIE:

Why not? Or you could come another time and ask Dr.
Cushman.—Tributary of the Weser. Five letters, the last
is an *e*.

BOLLIN:

Haven't the faintest idea. Never been in that part of the
country.—I suppose this influenza is very contagious?

SOPHIE:

And how! Microbes are no joke. But you wouldn't listen.
It wouldn't surprise me in the least if you'd caught it.—
Or over here. Thirty-seven down. I haven't anything in
that section. Nine letters: A Catholic order.

BOLLIN:

How many?

SOPHIE:

Nine.

BOLLIN (*counts on his fingers*):

Monstrance. It works.

SOPHIE:

Don't be silly.—I guess you're not a Catholic.

BOLLIN (*picks up Pinky*):

Oh yes I am. But that was a long time ago.—Say, that's not a bad idea. And docile. Handled systematically, might save a lot of work and trouble. Entries based on materials: celluloid, cloth, wood, rubber . . . (*Jumps up*) Will he be coming again today?

SOPHIE:

Not so close. Who?

BOLLIN:

The doctor, damn it.

SOPHIE:

That's not a nice way to talk.

BOLLIN:

Just tell me if he's coming.

SOPHIE:

What funny ideas you have! Do you think I'm the only pebble on the beach? They say it's a regular epidemic.

BOLLIN:

Then he can be crossed off.—And it's really so contagious that . . .

SOPHIE:

You're like my little brother. Always asking questions.

BOLLIN:

What would you expect of a cop?

SOPHIE:

Who's talking about Addi? The little imp will be three next Sunday, but he's got to know everything. Mummy, why is the man running? Mummy, what do automobiles eat? (*She takes off her glasses*) Imagine! The other day he wanted to know if robbers can get sick too. Isn't that funny? (*She giggles.* BOLLIN *jumps up and listens*)

BOLLIN:

Sh-sh. Isn't that something rattling?

SOPHIE:

Oh no, no! Oh, I'm so easily scared. Where? Where?

BOLLIN:

There it is. It's as plain as day.

SOPHIE:

Oh, I'm going to have to scream.

BOLLIN (*draws a revolver*):

I don't like to do this, it might backfire.

SOPHIE:

Oh that, now I hear it too. My, how you frightened me! That's Mummy. She's been shopping.

BOLLIN:

There's another detail that makes me sad. (*Aims at the door*)

SOPHIE (*laughing*):

You're really funny! You mustn't be afraid of Mummy. Mummy! Mummy! Come here.

MRS. DOMKE (*behind the door*):

Just a minute, child. I'm coming.

SOPHIE:

And bring me the new puzzle book.

MRS. DOMKE:

Have you finished with the old one?

SOPHIE:

It's too easy. It's boring.

MRS. DOMKE:

Always wanting something else. You're spoiled, child.

SOPHIE:

Honest. It only took me half an hour. Without an atlas.— Are you coming?

MRS. DOMKE (*looks through the crack in the door and sees* BOLLIN. *Her expression is friendly*):

Our little chatterbox seems to be better. (*She speaks to someone behind her*) No, you mayn't. No, you can't even peek. (*She shuts the door*) Ah, these children, these children!—Well?

SOPHIE:

The gentleman here is afraid.

MRS. DOMKE:

Really?—Good afternoon.

BOLLIN:

Afternoon. (BOLLIN *is embarrassed. He puts his revolver down on the bedside table*)

SOPHIE:

Guess who he's afraid of.

MRS. DOMKE:

My daughter says you're afraid. Pardon my curiosity, but may I ask whom you're afraid of?

SOPHIE:

You, you!

MRS. DOMKE:

That's impossible.

SOPHIE:

I'll have to tell Ella. He's afraid of Mummy.

MRS. DOMKE:

Seriously, young man? You're afraid of Mrs. Domke?

BOLLIN:

Call me Herman.

MRS. DOMKE:

Pleased to meet you.

SOPHIE:

I thought your name was Bollin?

BOLLIN:

But my first name is Herman.

MRS. DOMKE:

Pardon my curiosity. But where were you before? Before I went out shopping? It must have been about half an hour ago.

BOLLIN:

Before? Oh yes, before. Hm, where can I have been? That, my dear lady, is a long story.

SOPHIE:

How he beats about the bush! He was under the bed,
still as a mouse. And I didn't know a thing.

MRS. DOMKE:

My goodness! The whole time without moving?

SOPHIE:

I heard a little something. What can it be, I wondered.
The floor boards or the heating?

MRS. DOMKE:

Imagine! It serves you right if you had a little scare. It
was incredibly foolish of you. The child has a severe
case of flu. The doctor says she's on the mend, but even
so. (*She pulls* BOLLIN *away from the bed and whispers*)
There's been talk of closing the schools. Every day there
are new cases including some very bad ones. There was an
epidemic in 1917 when I was a child, I'll never forget it.
You never knew where it was going to strike next. It was
dreadful.—(*Aloud*) But gracious, you're standing. A sick
child makes a body forget her manners. Just a minute,
I'll . . .

BOLLIN:

Don't bother. I'll be moseying along. I just thought I'd
drop in. I've put you to too much trouble already. (*He
starts to leave*)

MRS. DOMKE:

I wouldn't hear of it. We have plenty of chairs.

SOPHIE:

And bring the puzzle book. I want to check the answers.—
(MRS. DOMKE *exits*) How do you like Mummy? The poor
thing talks quite a lot, doesn't she?

BOLLIN:

Think she'll keep the lid on?

SOPHIE:

What do you mean?

BOLLIN:

Your brother's in the cops, isn't he? Suppose she . . .

SOPHIE:

Wasn't she nice to you?

BOLLIN:

When you've got a suspicious nature like me . . .

SOPHIE:

After all Mummy's never laid eyes on you before.

BOLLIN:

That's just what I mean. (*Paces back and forth*) It would be pretty nice.—(*In an undertone*) The whole trouble is my sense of propriety. What makes me provide the press with photographs? This mania for showing my cards. Bollin in profile. Bollin full face.

SOPHIE (*takes off her glasses*):

See here. I wouldn't want to be indiscreet—Mummy always says: Don't keep asking personal questions. But all the same: Have you got something on your conscience?

BOLLIN:

Me?

SOPHIE:

You look tormented. Driven by some inner unrest. I never know where I'm at with you. One minute you're free and easy, you even laugh a little; the next you're all grumpy and clammed up.—Can't you stop pacing! Please.

BOLLIN:

I'm sorry. My legs do it all by themselves. There are reasons. Bad childhood experience. So now I pace.

SOPHIE:

I'm sorry. How was I to know?

BOLLIN:

A hard childhood leaves a mark.

SOPHIE:

Poor man!

BOLLIN:

Ah, when I think of it. The crowding. The smell. The

atmosphere. But even as a child I drew up tables: when peeling potatoes, for instance, the relation of the knife to the potato—width, thickness, and length of the peelings. Whole copybooks full. All lost in the war. But that's neither here nor there. My Uncle Max said: Hop down to the cellar and bring up some coal. So down I go, carefully counting the steps. Suspecting no harm. I was mostly thinking of my potato peels. So then when I . . .

SOPHIE:

Please stop. It must be a terrible story.

BOLLIN:

You're right. It was no picnic.

SOPHIE:

See!

BOLLIN:

I was only trying to brush in a self-portrait.

SOPHIE:

Another time, perhaps. But I'm sincerely sympathetic. I can see how a bad experience like that in early childhood might affect your whole life.

BOLLIN:

That's when I got on the wrong track. Who knows what I might have been if . . . My methodical leanings might have taken an entirely different. Besides, it was no fault of mine. Yes, I knew the kids. And I knew they hung out in the cellar, next to the laundry room. I knew they'd insulated the walls pretty well and I knew they had a band saw, glass wool, an enormous quantity of piano strings, and a big pile of bedsprings. See what I mean?

SOPHIE:

No! Please don't go on!

BOLLIN:

It was a Monday in January or February . . .

SOPHIE:

I sincerely beg you . . .

BOLLIN:

Anyway there was fire in the stoves . . .

SOPHIE (*pulls out the thermometer*):

Here! You wanted to know. And besides, Dr. Cushman said: No excitement. Well?

BOLLIN:

These details make me . . .

SOPHIE:

Gone up? A hundred and two and two-tenths? If only it's not a relapse. And I begged you. (*Starts to cry*)

BOLLIN:

Don't worry. It's nothing. It'll go down again. Would you like some more lemonade?

SOPHIE:

Thank you. (*She drinks*)—Mm, no, it's too much to ask of you.

BOLLIN:

What? What would you like me to do?

SOPHIE:

No, no, I really shouldn't. After all, I've only just met you and Mummy said . . .

BOLLIN:

But I'd be delighted to do you a little favor.

SOPHIE (*puts on her glasses*):

All right, I'll tell you. But don't hesitate to say no if you don't want to. (*Hands him a book*)

BOLLIN:

You want me to read to you?

SOPHIE:

Oh, I can see you don't feel like it.

BOLLIN:

That's not it. But I read pretty wretchedly.

SOPHIE:

Oh, please! That's just what I like. People that read any old way.

BOLLIN:

What would you like? This one, the story of Faithful John? Or this one: The Robber Bridegroom?

SOPHIE:

Better read the one about Faithful John. I'm afraid the other might work me up like your childhood memories. Incidentally, you may call me Sophie.

MRS. DOMKE (*in the doorway*):

No no no! That won't do! I'm sorry, young man, but I shall have to be severe with you. And you should be more thoughtful too, Sophie. First all that time under the bed and now sitting so close. There's no sense in playing the he-man. Mr. Wanka upstairs is a skilled ditchdigger. He's exposed to all kinds of weather day in day out, he ought to be hardened. Well, he's been in bed for the last two weeks. And what has he got? The flu. And how did he get it? At a shop meeting. Which shows you that even the strongest men have their weak spots.—Here, child, your puzzle book.

BOLLIN:

The little girl wanted me to read to her. You mustn't be angry, Mrs. . . .

MRS. DOMKE:

Domke. My husband was in Schichau. Not in the dock-yards, in the office. He was always bragging about his good health too. He'd just celebrated his twenty-fifth year with the . . .

BOLLIN:

My sincerest sympathy.

MRS. DOMKE:

It was three years ago last December. Our little Conny was the last thing he did for us. Oh well, I suppose it had to be. But goodness, I stand here talking when I ought to be winding my wool. What do you think, child? Maybe I could ask our visitor to help me for just a few minutes.

SOPHIE:

Oh, Mummy!

BOLLIN:

But I'd be glad to. I'd have been glad to read too. But I wasn't allowed. (MRS. DOMKE *arranges the chairs*)

SOPHIE:

Maybe later, when I'm through with the puzzle.

MRS. DOMKE:

Will you be sensible!—That's fine. (BOLLIN *holds the wool*, MRS. DOMKE *winds*) Hold it good and loose. That's it. Now relax. Follow along with your shoulders. Where could you have learned to do it so nicely? Your mother must have taught you.

BOLLIN:

I've always liked to do monotonous things.

MRS. DOMKE:

That's a great virtue and very unusual.

BOLLIN:

Repetition is the key to knowledge.

MRS. DOMKE:

Would you mind turning just a little?

BOLLIN:

The law of series is my guiding principle.

MRS. DOMKE:

Just a teeny bit more. You've got to be straight across from me.

BOLLIN:

Statistics never lie. Everything we do proves it.

MRS. DOMKE:

That's a funny thing. If you weren't sitting right here, I'd think . .

BOLLIN:

Every detail . . . It's a little warm in here.

MRS. DOMKE:

It has to be. The doctor said to keep up a good fire. Isn't it odd, Sophie child, I could swear I'd seen Mr. Bollin somewhere.

SOPHIE:

I can't listen now, Mummy. Nineteen down: Undecided game. Four letters.

BOLLIN:

Draw. D-r-a-w.

SOPHIE:

It fits, Mummy, it fits.

MRS. DOMKE:

How nicely the two of you work together. But even with no one to help her the child can solve the knottiest puzzles. What was I . . . ? Oh yes. I must have seen you somewhere.

BOLLIN:

If I may say so, that seems rather unlikely. I don't live here.

MRS. DOMKE:

Don't you have something to do with the movies?

BOLLIN:

No use racking your brains. Lots of people look like me.

MRS. DOMKE:

A little higher, please.—Ah, now it comes back to me. You're an athlete. Come along now. Tell me the truth.

BOLLIN:

Well, occasionally, when I get a chance.

MRS. DOMKE:

And I saw you in the paper, this big.

BOLLIN:

I don't subscribe to a clipping service.

MRS. DOMKE:

You're just too modest.

BOLLIN:

Well, I may have been in the paper once.

MRS. DOMKE:

There!—Don't you remember, child? I showed you. I think it was the Sunday paper.

BOLLIN:

Wednesday, January 12th.

MRS. DOMKE:

Are you sure?—Well, you should know best.

SOPHIE (*takes off her glasses*):

I'm not getting anywhere.

MRS. DOMKE:

Mustn't be so impatient.—Perhaps Mr. Bollin will give you the benefit of his wide experience.

BOLLIN:

I don't like to put my foot in it.

MRS. DOMKE:

Always so modest.

BOLLIN:

They may ask questions that would make me sad.

SOPHIE:

I bet you don't know either. A writ authorizing an officer to make an arrest.

MRS. DOMKE:

Hm. How many letters?

SOPHIE:

Seven. The third from the last ought to be an *a*.

MRS. DOMKE:

Well, Mr. Bollin? What do you say?

SOPHIE:

I know you know. I can see by your face. Please.

BOLLIN:

That's a tough one.—Why don't you wait till you have the other letters?

MRS. DOMKE:

You don't know our Sophie. The child won't leave you a moment's peace until she has it all worked out.

SOPHIE:

If Addi were here, he'd know right off.

BOLLIN:

The traffic cop! (*He gives a start*)

MRS. DOMKE:

Careful, young man, my wool!—Should I call him up? Maybe he's at headquarters by now.

BOLLIN:

Wait! Just a second.

SOPHIE:

That's the way. Oh, Mummy, I love it when everybody joins in. And if Mr. Bollin doesn't know, we'll call up Addi.

BOLLIN:

Seven letters?

SOPHIE:

Exactly.

BOLLIN:

And the third from last is an *a*?

SOPHIE:

Oh, it's so exciting. With the telephone and . . .

BOLLIN:

Warrant!—Write it down. I said warrant. And what's the next? We wouldn't want to stop there.

SOPHIE:

It fits. It fits. Isn't that funny! I'd never have thought of it. W-a-r-rant.

MRS. DOMKE:

I had a hazy idea. They really shouldn't put these technical terms in a crossword puzzle. Luckily, we had you. Mr. Bollin·is so well informed. Thank him, Sophie. I'd never have expected an athlete to be so clever, and so sweet too.

SOPHIE:

Oh, Mummy!—You mustn't mind Mummy. She says the weirdest things. But she's really the dearest thing in the world. (*She lies down*)

BOLLIN:

She's mighty lucky. Wish I'd had a mother like you.

MRS. DOMKE:

Are you an orphan?

BOLLIN:

Yes, on both sides. All I've got is an uncle somewhere. The watch here and my fountain pen are from him.

MRS. DOMKE:

They must be very valuable.—And aside from your uncle? I mean, you're young, handsome, well mannered.

BOLLIN:

Goodness, what can I say?

MRS. DOMKE:

So there.

BOLLIN:

It's not the way you think. I'm alone most of the time.

MRS. DOMKE:

If you're a stranger here, you're likely to meet the wrong kind of people. And didn't you say you came from out of town?

BOLLIN:

It's all very hard on me. In fact, when you come right down to it, it's sad. My Uncle Max felt the same way. Once you commit yourself to a cause, a system, or to be specific, the law of series, you're doomed to solitude. I get along nicely with children.—Ah, too bad! The wool's all finished.

MRS. DOMKE:

Isn't it a pity? We might have gone on for hours. Do you

know what? Come and see us again. How about Sunday? It's our Conny's birthday. And let's hope our Sophie will be better by then.—She's sleeping. The puzzle must have tired her. Sh-sh, quiet! At four for coffee?

BOLLIN:

If you really want me.

MRS. DOMKE:

I'd be delighted.

BOLLIN:

The pleasure is all mine.

MRS. DOMKE:

And don't you dare to bring anything.

BOLLIN:

Oh, come, come.

MRS. DOMKE:

But now I'm going to give you something.

BOLLIN:

You really shouldn't.

MRS. DOMKE:

You take it before you go to bed. An ounce of prevention. We wouldn't want you to get sick. (*They tiptoe to the door.* MRS. DOMKE *points*) You've left your thingamajig on the table.

BOLLIN:

One of these days I'll forget my head. That's what comes of winding wool.

MRS. DOMKE (*pretending to threaten him*):

Oh, yes. That's how it often begins. (*They laugh in an undertone and give each other familiar little pokes*) Anyway you'd have found it on Sunday. Addi, my oldest boy, knows all about those things. He'd have taken good care of it.

BOLLIN (*tiptoes to the bedside table, pockets the revolver and Pinky, and tiptoes back*):

Here we are again.

E

MRS. DOMKE:

Do you always carry it around with you?

BOLLIN:

I only go without it on holidays.

MRS. DOMKE:

Ah, a man of principle!

BOLLIN:

My Uncle Max was the same way.

MRS. DOMKE:

And my husband always kept a little tin fire engine in his pocket. We all have our ways. (*They leave the room.* SOPHIE *sits up and reaches for her glasses*)

SOPHIE:

How quietly he can walk.—He was right next to the bed before I heard him breathing.—If only he hasn't caught it. (*She puts on the glasses and searches on the bedside table*) Where can she be? She was here a minute ago.— Pinky. Pinky! Why did he take my Pinky?

CURTAIN

Act II

Prologue

*(In front of the curtain.—*BOLLIN *is sitting on a chair. On the floor, beside the chair, stands a telephone.* BOLLIN *has the doll Pinky on his lap and is playing with her. Under the chair a pile of folders)*

BOLLIN:

You want more? Always the little glutton!—*(He holds the doll to his ear)* Is that so? Again?—Well, all right, but this is the last time. *(He stands up, puts the doll on a chair, takes a long knife out of his pocket, and makes a sinister face)* My name is Bollin. What, you don't know me, my much too lovely young lady? Don't you read the papers? Observe me carefully, I'll show you how affectionate Bollin can be. *(He screams and thrusts the knife into the doll's belly)* Sawdust!—Well, Pinky, are you satisfied? *(He carefully wipes the knife, takes needle and thread, and sews up the cut)* We mustn't do this too often, you know. Twice a week at the very most.—Now what is it? Pinky, you're insatiable. Wouldn't you rather play tag or postman?—What a stubborn thing you are! It's always got to be knifing or shooting, you're just not interested in anything else. *(He stands up, pulls down a hook suspended from the ceiling, and hangs the doll on it)* All right, Pinky, but you'll have to stop squinting. Remember our agreement. It's so irritating.—Fifteen feet. *(He paces off the distance, takes a military attitude, and draws an air pistol)* Three shots will be fired with the unsupported left hand from a distance of fifteen feet. Load and cock. Fire at will! *(He fires)* Missed, missed,

101

missed. Three misses. But it's your fault. Didn't I ask you to look at me in a normal way?—All right for you, turn around. You've asked for it. (*He turns the doll around, paces off the distance again, and loads*) Don't get that offended look. You know perfectly well that I've got to finish the exercise. Three shots will be fired with the unsupported right hand from a distance of fifteen feet. Load and cock. Fire at will. (*He fires*) That's better! Unload weapon. Exercise concluded.—You could have had it in front. (*He unhooks the doll and examines its back. Imitating an officer's voice*) Excellent, Bollin. Keep up the good work.—Did you hear that, Pinky? It may mean advancement.—Yes, sir, I'll do my best.—Dismissed.— He said I should keep up the good work.

(*The telephone rings,* BOLLIN *picks up the receiver*)

Bollin. Who?—Hm, hm. (*To the doll*) A young man, an admirer.—What have you got to show?—Pardon?—That's no good, it's unmethodical. (*To the doll*) He wants to study with me.—See here, my young friend, if you want to get anywhere in this profession, don't be a slavish imitator. Be yourself! Think up an idea. My Uncle Max always said: Ideas, luminous moments, flashes of genius. Ring me up again when you get a flash. (*He hangs up*) I guess I told him off. What was his name again?—Erwin Whatshisname. (*He gives the doll a long, thoughtful look*) I'm too old to be playing with dolls.—And I ought to change my methods. Piddling imitators are getting wise to my tricks. The illustrated weeklies are beginning to make me offers. Anyway I ought to do something about my health. The city air is murder. The flu is spreading. Good-by, Pinky. I'm going to the country, to the woods. Bollin is going to take a look at nature.

CURTAIN

The Cuckoo

(*An evergreen forest. A cross section of the mound in the center of the stage shows a pit.* BOLLIN *covers the pit with branches. When he is finished, he trots to the left side of the stage and makes a few quick changes in his dress, by way of imitating his future victim*)

BOLLIN:

I don't know a thing.—I'm walking along. Thinking no evil.—Walking along, suspecting nothing, thinking of something pleasant. (*He approaches the pit*) My eyes are glued to the ground. My senses keen and alert, stirred by the suspicion that goes with my calling. (*He stands at the edge of the pit, lifts one foot to take the fateful step*) If someone came along, someone else, knowing nothing, thinking no evil but on the contrary, in spite of his keen, alert senses and the suspicion that goes with his calling, thinking of something pleasant, he'd take this step—but not I. I should say not! Perhaps I could move this little branch, like this, and over here I could remove the traces of my passion for order. (*He makes some slight changes in the arrangement of the branches and inspects his work with satisfaction*) It would be easy to fall in love with my own work. Dangerous trains of thought, luring me . . . almost . . . into the abyss. I'd actually let myself be lured—but duty holds me back, calling with its old familiar voice: Not yet, Bollin, not yet. The law still needs you. The series is still incomplete. (*He jumps across the pit, hops about among the trees, and cries out to the left*) Cuckoo, cuckoo . . . cuckoo . . .

A VOICE:

Cuckoo!

BOLLIN:

Cuckoo!

A VOICE:

Cuckoo . . . cuckoo! (*The bearded, pipe-smoking fores-*
ter comes in from the left)

BOLLIN:

Cuckoo!

FORESTER:

Cuckoo! (*He approaches the pit, stands briefly at the edge,*
examines the ground suspiciously, bends down . . .)

BOLLIN:

Cuckoo, cuckoo, cuckoo!

(*The* FORESTER *straightens up, follows the cuckoo call,*
and falls into the pit, dropping his rifle and game bag.
BOLLIN *pops out from behind the tree, rubbing his hands*
gleefully, slings the rifle and game bag over his shoulder,
and looks into the pit)

FORESTER (*drawing at his pipe, which has gone out*):
Bollin?

BOLLIN:

Cuckoo!

FORESTER:

It won't draw. (*Knocks out his pipe*) Are you Bollin? Just
tell me that.

BOLLIN:

With a capital *B* and two *ll*'s. (*Hangs the rifle and the*
bag on a branch)

FORESTER:

Just as I thought.—But where's . . . ? (*He rummages in*
his pockets. BOLLIN *opens the game bag*)

BOLLIN:

In case you're looking for your notebook and the pencil
that goes with it, here you are. (*He passes them down into*
the pit) I'm taking notes too. (*Writes in his notebook*)

FORESTER (*writing*):
With a *B* and two *ll*'s. Residence?

BOLLIN:

Write that he's engaged in moving. I'll write: Took the step, and the time of day. (*Takes out his watch*)

FORESTER:

Engaged in moving.—Motive?

BOLLIN:

Change of air.

FORESTER:

For reasons of health?

BOLLIN:

You've guessed it, the city was undermining my constitution.

FORESTER:

And now you're undermining the security of my district.

BOLLIN:

Cuckoo!

FORESTER:

Why would you want to do that?

BOLLIN:

Cuckoo!

FORESTER:

Answer me, Bollin! I haven't seen hair nor hide of my two assistants for the last three weeks. And Forester Platzmann of Melchow has disappeared too.

BOLLIN:

The law of series has been confirmed.

FORESTER:

Vanished without trace.

BOLLIN:

Forester Platzmann also felt impelled to move. Change of air.

FORESTER:

Don't joke.

BOLLIN:

A pious man! He certainly deserved a little place upstairs.

FORESTER:

Too young, Bollin, think of it, thirty-five, that's no proper age.

BOLLIN:

He'll have plenty of time to grow moss up there. Heaven must be divided up into forest districts too.

FORESTER:

His place was down here! Don't play God, you have no right. I don't know what trade you may have learned, but you certainly don't know anything about forestry.

BOLLIN:

I don't like foresters.

FORESTER:

Nobody made you leave the city.

BOLLIN:

I regard them as superfluous. My statistics prove it.

FORESTER:

Oho! And what about the criminals of the forest?—the poachers, the firebugs, the resin thieves, the poachers, and . . . more poachers?

BOLLIN:

There wouldn't be any if there weren't any foresters.

FORESTER:

I'll have to make a note of that. There wouldn't . . .

BOLLIN:

It's very wise of you to take that sentence down. I've devoted a great deal of thought to the matter. Here. My little book speaks volumes.

FORESTER:

Fiddlesticks, intellectual nonsense. You're an incurable idealist, a revolutionary, a Red. Destructive, pessimistic to the core. An out-and-out nihilist—hm. And what does our intellectual friend do? He sets himself up as a judge.

If there were no foresters there wouldn't be any . . .
That's preposterous. And I'm ready to wager that you
can't tell a rabbit from a rocking horse.

BOLLIN:

Distinctions. Why should I draw distinctions?

FORESTER:

For purposes of orientation. Or just to learn, to evaluate,
to form a picture. It never hurt anyone to round out his
knowledge, to fill in the gaps.—For instance, you go
roaming through the woods, you lurk in wait for con-
scientious foresters—but can you tell me the names of
these trees?

BOLLIN:

Trees? Did you say trees? Where, what trees?

FORESTER:

Let me out and I'll explain our forest to you.

BOLLIN:

That doesn't fall in with my plans. Why would I have
done all this work? My hands are full of blisters. My shirt
is sticky with sweat. And you? You go bumming around the
landscape, absolutely superfluous in your green uniform,
and now you want to deprive me of my hard-earned re-
ward—you're an exploiter, that's what you are, a slave
driver!

FORESTER:

Nonsense, Bollin, nobody wants you to do anything.
My men will fill in the hole, you won't be prosecuted,
you have my solemn promise—and think of the education
you'll get. I'll teach you the secrets of the forest.

BOLLIN:

What good will that do me?

FORESTER:

So that's the lay of the land. He despises nature.

BOLLIN:

Not at all. Listen to this: Cuckoo!

FORESTER:

You can't even imitate a simple bird call. This is the mouth position: Cuckoo!

BOLLIN:

That's what I said: Cuckoo!

FORESTER:

Wrong! Cuckoo!

BOLLIN:

Cuckoo! Cuckoo! Cuckoo!

FORESTER:

I give up. You'll never learn.

BOLLIN:

It's good enough. You fell for my cuckoo, didn't you? Cuckoo! (*He jumps over the pit and takes a shovel from behind the trees*) Now may I ask a simple question?

FORESTER:

Let's not have any false modesty. As long as a man keeps asking questions, he has hope and good will. What would you like to know, Bollin? I know, you're not interested in trees. Maybe I could tell you something about our native birds or about forest ants or bark beetles?—Well?

BOLLIN:

Do you know what a shovel is?

FORESTER (*after a pause*):

Go ahead, I've had my say.

BOLLIN:

Not a spade. A shovel.

FORESTER:

Go ahead! Show old Greensward all the wonderful things you can do with a shovel.

BOLLIN:

It's not so much.—Always the same: Cuckoo, cuckoo, and so on.

FORESTER:

All the same, I'm curious. What forester can afford to be buried under his own trees?

BOLLIN:

It's all the same to the trees.

FORESTER:

Oh no, I'm sure you're wrong about that. A proper forest knows its keeper.

BOLLIN:

Pure imagination! Only a forester could dream up such nonsense.—I've inspected some of these tree trunks very carefully. They don't give a damn about people.

FORESTER (*smugly*):

My spruces know me!

BOLLIN:

Let's be realistic, Greensward, and stick to the facts. Who pays you? The trees or the government?

FORESTER:

Both have rewarded me in their own way.

BOLLIN:

Bah, he doesn't know one thing about nature and he calls himself a forester.

FORESTER:

Anyway I can imitate a cuckoo call a damn sight better than you—and I know my district inside out.

BOLLIN:

And now you'll really get to the bottom of it. (*He laughs scornfully*)

FORESTER:

Let's get started.

BOLLIN:

Have you a last wish?

FORESTER:

My pipe's gone out. I must have lost my game bag when I fell.

BOLLIN:

What! Here in the middle of the woods, you want to . . . ?

FORESTER:

Just one little pipe.

BOLLIN:

I saw a sign a little while ago. Said something about certain things being prohibited.

FORESTER:

That's only for hikers and berry pickers.

BOLLIN:

And your laws allow for exceptions?

FORESTER:

Greatness, Bollin, has always been an exception.

BOLLIN:

Oh, all right, it's not my woods. If you promise to be careful. (*He takes a lighter from the game bag and tosses it into the pit*) But you'll be responsible! (*The* FORESTER *lights his pipe and smokes*) Be that as it may, your inconsistency deserves to be noted. (*Writes*)

FORESTER (*after a short pause*):

Bollin!

BOLLIN:

Hm?

FORESTER:

My rifle!

BOLLIN:

It's doing fine up here.

FORESTER:

You're sure it's not lying in the sand?

BOLLIN:

I've put it in a safe place.

FORESTER:

That's very kind of you. Can I have it?

BOLLIN:

Your gun?

FORESTER:

It's not loaded.

BOLLIN:

A gun's a gun.

FORESTER:

You can look in the chamber. It's empty.

BOLLIN:

Loaded or not, it's a matter of principle.

FORESTER:

Mightn't this be the exception that proves . . .

BOLLIN:

I'm not even listening. You obey your laws, I abide by mine. As my Uncle Max said: You go out the way you came in.

FORESTER:

I'd like to hold it.

BOLLIN:

That's a lot of sentimentality.

FORESTER:

It's been my companion for almost twenty years.

BOLLIN:

Then it's high time for you to part.

FORESTER:

We're so attached to each other.

BOLLIN:

That's just what I meant: dependence. Time to break with the old habits. The gun stays up there, Greensward stays down there . . .

FORESTER:

Twenty years!

BOLLIN:

We mustn't cling to earthly things. Man should be free, without ballast!

FORESTER:

But my gun . . .

BOLLIN:

You can't take it with you.—Well, all right, I'll shovel in a layer, about up to your belt, and then I'll hand it down.—Now are you satisfied?

FORESTER:

Thank you, Bollin, thank you and—good hunting!

BOLLIN (*picking up the shovel*):

If I were a cynic, I'd say good fishing—with St. Peter.

FORESTER (*smiling*):

Oh, you're alluding to those wormlike parasites?

(*Bollin begins shoveling earth into the pit.* SLICK *and* SPRAT *enter from the left. They are carrying baskets filled with blueberries: they set down their baskets at the edge of the pit*)

SLICK:

D'you know this guy?

SPRAT:

Him or him?

SLICK:

Everybody knows him. I mean the other one.

SPRAT:

Course I know him. It's old Greensward. (*The* FORESTER *jumps up.* BOLLIN *stands leaning on his shovel*)

SLICK:

Looks like he's getting buried.

SPRAT:

High time.—Like some blueberries, Grampa? (*She tosses some blueberries into the pit*)

FORESTER:

Bollin! Chase those brats away.

BOLLIN:

Kids don't bother me. Never have.

FORESTER:

They have no permit to pick berries.

BOLLIN:

Who cares?

FORESTER:

They upset me. They put me in the wrong frame of mind.

BOLLIN:

Did you hear that, children? Mr. Greensward wants peace and quiet.

SPRAT:

Hell, he never gave us any peace and quiet.

SLICK:

He was always playing the ogre, rolling his eyes like he'd stepped out of the fairy tale and we was those kids, you know the ones, mister . . .

BOLLIN:

Hänsel and Gretel if I'm not mistaken.

SPRAT:

Thanks, mister.

FORESTER:

I appeal to your sense of decorum. Get rid of the children.

BOLLIN:

All right, beat it.—You can come back when the law's been carried out, and help stamp down the sand.

SLICK:

Come on, Sprat.

SPRAT:

I want to watch.

SLICK:

It's interesting. It don't happen every day.

SPRAT:

Say, Grampa Greensward, they're swiping firewood on Pigeon Hill.

SLICK:

And in Cotter's Hollow.

SPRAT:

With a handcart.

SLICK:

And there wasn't just brushwood in it, there was something underneath.

SPRAT:

Something brown with a little short tail . . .

SLICK:

. . . and long ears.

FORESTER:

Bollin!

BOLLIN:

That's enough now, leave him alone.

SPRAT:

Aw go on. That's the kind of stuff he's interested in. That's his job.

SLICK:

And we almost forgot the best part: There's a big cloud of smoke over Swedesleap.

SPRAT:

Some durn fool dropped a match.

SLICK:

Right where it's so dry.

BOLLIN:

You mustn't tell him such things. It pains him.

SPRAT:

I spose he never pained me?—Go on, Slick, tell him what old Greensward done to me.

SLICK:

Yeah, he gave her a licking.

SPRAT:

I still got the marks.

FORESTER:

Because they were in the nursery.

SPRAT:

Nuts! I spose I can tell my mother that? (*She points to*

the baskets) No berries today, Ma, we're not allowed to pick in the nursery.

SLICK:

I guess he thinks we come out here for the fun of it.

FORESTER:

Oh, these city children! Maybe once a year they go to the zoo, and that's all they know about nature.

SPRAT:

And we can't even go there any more, 'cause we been evacuated.

SLICK:

It was better back home.

SPRAT:

There ain't even any lions around here.

SLICK:

Or a baboon or a decent kangaroo from Australia.

FORESTER:

Bollin!

SLICK:

Don't bother with him.

SPRAT:

I'd have filled him in long ago.

BOLLIN (*to the* FORESTER):

Well, what do you want now?

SPRAT:

Why don't you shovel, mister?

SLICK:

I wouldn't wait if I were you.

SPRAT:

You gonna change your mind?

BOLLIN:

Pipe down.—What is it, Greensward?

FORESTER:

You've buried my two assistants and Platzmann, haven't you?

BOLLIN:

Cuckoo—and no more Platzmann.

FORESTER:

Yes, I can see it all. But let me ask you this, did they have a peaceful time of it, or, or . . .

BOLLIN:

It was blissfully quiet. Platzmann even dropped off to sleep before he was half covered.

FORESTER:

And the assistants?

BOLLIN:

Just a second. I'll check. (*Opens his notebook*) Oh well, at first they were a little restless . . . they were so young, you know, they were afraid of missing something—but then they pulled themselves together. It was all very awe-inspiring, like a church.

FORESTER (*in a loud voice*):

Aha! Awe-inspiring . . . church—well, haven't I got the same rights? Why all this noise, these voices? (*More softly*) I beg you, Bollin. The only sound I want to hear is your shovel. The good Baltic sand, maybe a bird now and then and the wind in the spruces.

SPRAT:

See, he said spruces.—They are spruces, ain't they, Grampa Greensward?

FORESTER:

My spruces!

SPRAT:

He always calls 'em pines.

FORESTER:

Heaven help us. Those city schools! What do the children learn?

SLICK:

Anyway they're c-c-conifers.

FORESTER:

Isn't it awful, Bollin? Such ignorance! But you don't care anything about our glorious nature either.

BOLLIN:

Well, I know they're conifers too, I've noticed the cones.

FORESTER (*with bitterness*):

Conifers.—That's the whole family. One genus, the pine for instance . . .

SLICK:

See, pine is right. There are pines.

FORESTER:

Why, naturally, children. But not here, anyway not the true pine. There are many different varieties of pine. The Scotch pine, for instance, grows almost exclusively in mountainous regions. It has sharp square needles and pendent cones. The wood is used for fuel, but also for cheap furniture. The resin is drawn off and used for making turpentine.

SLICK:

That's interesting, Sprat, isn't it?

SPRAT:

But these here are spruces.

FORESTER:

Not so fast. We'll come to them. First we'll finish up with the pine. What was I saying?

SLICK:

Turpentine.

FORESTER:

Right. But also cellulose, excelsior, pine needle extract . . .

SLICK:

What about oil?

FORESTER:

Splendid, child. And you put it in the bathtub, don't you?

SPRAT:

We haven't got any.

FORESTER:

Maybe Mr. Bollin has one?

BOLLIN:

I might mention pine needle salts.

FORESTER:

Excellent! Aren't you the sly one! I've a hunch you know more about nature than you like to admit.

BOLLIN:

Don't make me laugh. I just happened to know that. Once in a while I buy a little package. It's supposed to be good for you. And now and then I like to relax in the privacy of my bath.

SPRAT:

And now tell us about the spruces.

SLICK:

We've heard all about pines.

FORESTER:

I think we'll need a little patience. The children . . . (*With a sweeping gesture* BOLLIN *gives his permission*) Run along now. Mr. Bollin has no objection. Pick up a few spruce cones and throw them down.

SLICK:

Right away! (*He quickly gathers some cones and throws them into the pit*)

FORESTER:

Stop, that's plenty.

SPRAT:

But how can you see anything in that hole?

SLICK:

He's going to ruin his eyes.

SPRAT:

He's trying to see with his lighter.

FORESTER:

The visibility is indeed very poor.

SPRAT:

Can't you tell us by heart?

SLICK:

Don't be silly. He wants to make it visual. Let him come up a minute!

SPRAT (*to* BOLLIN):

Hey, mister, leave him up.

SLICK:

He can't do anything down there.

BOLLIN:

Is that another one of your ideas, Greensward? Are you trying to make use of the children just to get another breath of fresh air?

FORESTER:

Certainly not. I've wound up my accounts. It's only these children's thirst for knowledge—they want me to explain the little secrets of the forest.

BOLLIN:

Can't you do it down there?

SPRAT:

It's too dark, mister. Cantcha see that?

SLICK:

He'll go back down when he's finished.

BOLLIN:

He explained all that other stuff . . . about the pines . . . very nicely down there.

SPRAT:

Naturally, 'cause there ain't none here and Slick wouldn't believe there ain't none here but only in the . . .

SLICK:

Anyway his spiel made sense.

SPRAT:

But we ain't on pines any more, we're on spruces.

FORESTER:

I'm not trying to talk you into anything. But shouldn't we educate these children a little? In the city I'm sure they seldom get such an opportunity to learn about our native conifers.

SLICK:

We have a Christmas tree every year.

SPRAT:

We don't. My mother always says they shed too bad and the carpet's still full of needles at Easter and the skeleton's still cluttering up the balcony.

FORESTER:

Well, what do you say?

BOLLIN:

It's against my law, it's a violation that I'll have to enter in my record, but all right, he can come up a second. (*He gives the* FORESTER *his hand and pulls him out of the pit. The* FORESTER *slaps the sand off his jacket.* SPRAT *helps him.* BOLLIN *writes in his notebook*)

SPRAT:

Gimme a hand, Slick.

SLICK:

It'll only get dirty again.

FORESTER:

Ah yes, the good Baltic sand. Well then, let's begin with the sand. It's the only soil our spruce will grow in.

SLICK:

Why?

FORESTER:

It's frugal, a true child of these Baltic shores. It's not a fine wood, but still the spruce is a useful, important tree. It has a spreading root and can be put to very much the same uses as the pine.

SLICK:

But it doesn't grow in the mountains.

FORESTER:

Oh yes, a related species does. In the mountainous regions of Europe, near the timber line, we have the dwarf spruce or miniature spruce.

SLICK:

Dwarf spruce is wild.

SPRAT:

Why dwarf?

FORESTER:

Well, in those regions the weather conditions are entirely different, tall slender trees like this wouldn't be viable. For that reason the dwarf spruce . . .

SPRAT:

. . . dwarf spruce! (*The* FORESTER *takes his game bag*)

FORESTER:

. . . also known as the miniature spruce . . . (*He takes his gun*)

SPRAT *and* SLICK:

. . . miniature spruce!

FORESTER:

Or midget spruce . . .

SPRAT *and* SLICK:

Midget spruce!

FORESTER:

. . . is small in stature and has a stunted bushlike appearance. Let's go through it again. For that reason the . . . ?

SPRAT *and* SLICK:

. . . dwarf spruce!

FORESTER:

Also known as the miniature spruce . . . (*They exit*)

SPRAT *and* SLICK:

Miniature spruce.

FORESTER:

. . . or midget spruce . . .

SPRAT *and* SLICK:

   . . . or midget spruce is small in stature . . .

   (BOLLIN *looks after them, writes in his notebook, spits on his hands, and begins to fill in the pit. Several cuckoo calls are heard in the distance*)

BOLLIN (*leaning on his shovel*):

   Cuckoo! Cuckoo!

   (*After waiting some time in vain for the cuckoo to answer, he goes on shoveling*)

CURTAIN

Act III

Prologue

(BOLLIN *sits facing a Christmas tree. He looks unshaven.
Next to the tree a telephone. A filing cabinet with folders.*
BOLLIN *leafs through a folder, throws it down*)

BOLLIN:

Incomplete series. Documented inconsistency. Conifers!—
I shouldn't have got mixed up with them. For today I
ask: What is nature to Bollin?—I'm a city man. My
records prove it. The usual butcher boys would be better.
Or postmen? Why not? But Christmas trees? Then why
not Santa Clauses? There are two of them sweating outside every department store. (*Knocks the silver tip off the
tree*) But the season is too short. Yes, it's been starting
in November lately, but even so. (*Smashes one decoration
after another*) Leaves no time for proper planning. By
the third Sunday in Advent I'd be reduced to improvisa-
tion. Though the change-over from foresters to this occupational group . . . Yes, yes, self-criticism is in order:
I might have stuck to foresters. After the Greensward
incident I could have moved my theater of operations.
Different trees, different foresters. I might have tried an
oak wood, I might have gathered beechnuts, there are all
sorts of forests. And what of the heath with its heather
and birches?—Too late! Experiment ruined. Series broken
off. I wanted to rid the world of foresters. And the foresters
fouled me up.

(*Takes an ax and chops the branches off the tree*)

Chop it down! Saw it up! Off with its beard! Shave it!
(*He gives a start, lets the tree fall*) Sh-a-ve? Wait a second.

123

Shave? Right! Barbers! Why, of course! Cool smooth fingers. Talk into the mirror. Cough into combs. (*The telephone rings.* BOLLIN *picks up the receiver*) Stare at the part in your hair. Hello. Who?—Hi, Erwin.—What's that? If I'm in town again? Can you hear me? That's right, wound up. Nothing more to be gained. Nonsense. So that's what the papers are saying? Let them. They always know so much. Yes, yes, I know. The illustrated weeklies live on me.—What? With you? How many times do I have to? No. It doesn't appeal to me. It still doesn't. I believe you, Erwin, I know it would appeal to you. But it can't be done. I've got to make my way alone. Maybe later, if I try mixed series. Call again. Good-by.—(*He hangs up and leafs hastily through the phone book*) Barbers. Barbers. That young whippersnapper. Wants to latch on. Fresh out of college and wants to cash in.— *B, b, ba,* barbers.—Sociological study: Group Murder and the Labor Market. All right, let him sponge if he wants to, but not on me. Adeloth, Karlheinz, Ladies and Gentlemen, Bischofsberg 28, city's leading establishment.—Well, that remains to be seen. (*He picks up a new folder and writes in it*) No more boy scout stuff. No more hiking through the greenery. Do I look like a wood sprite? A new file is hereby opened. Uncle Max would be proud of me. His fountain pen will be kept busy. (*Jumps up*) From now on Bollin will get a shave twice a week.

CURTAIN

The Prima Donna

(*The drawing room of the soprano* MIMI LANDELLA. *On the right a divan. In the center background a gilt bathtub with a canopy over it. Beside it a screen. To the left an overloaded dressing table.* MIMI LANDELLA, *the* PRIMA DONNA, *is lying on the divan. In the middle of the room*

*a photographer behind an old-fashioned camera on a tri-
pod. The photographer's head and shoulders are covered
by a black cloth. He is holding a flash lamp*)

PRIMA DONNA:

Closer, camera boy! Still closer. (Do you think Landella is
lying here with a book, immersed in her reading, for the
fun of it?) (*She reads. Flash. She jumps up, throws the
book down, turns the photographer toward the bathtub*)
Now listen carefully, Bodokins. This is going to be gently
whimsical: the fountain nymph. Mihmihmihmih . . .
Bodo, my voice is gone.—Mih. Miiih. Mihmihmihmiiih.
It's back again.—Now! Thy nymph! (*She sits down dec-
oratively on the edge of the bathtub, turns on the faucet,
holds her hand under the stream of water, and takes the
pose of a nymph*) Does it come across, my little Neptune?
—Okay! *Flash. She jumps up, runs through the room
with waving towel, piping the notes of an aria from*
Rheingold) And now my entrance. (Goblin, raven of
Wotan, give heed. Your hour has struck! You will have
the privilege, the distinction, the good fortune to witness
Landella's grand entrance. You are about to take a picture
that will immortalize something to which no picture can
do justice. (*Warbling silvery notes, she disappears behind
the screen*)
Keep your flashlight in readiness. Falter not, O Raven.
Landella's entrance. (*With a shrill cry she leaps through
the paper screen. Flash*) Too late. I knew it: too late. How
could I ever pick this dwarf to witness my grand entrance!
Wretch! Beast of the caverns! (*Through the torn screen
enters* BOLLIN, *carefully groomed. He is carrying a metal
suitcase in his left hand*) How could I take up with this
tired camera boy who flashes a fraction of a second too
late! Don't you dare to come out. Stay in your black hole.
After all I've suffered must I look on wretchedness?—
My fiancé. Ha! I engage myself to a photographer. And
what does he do: He flashes too late. (*Loudly*) Too late!
(*Softly*) Too late. (*She stands before the mirror and*

musses her hair. Little shrill screams. BOLLIN *approaches slowly. The photographer trembles*)

Idiot! Idiot! Idio . . . (*She sees* BOLLIN *in the mirror. Whispers*) Bollin! Mirror, mirror on the wall, don't deceive me. Is it a dream? Oh, sweet image! Are you merely a figment of desire? Has the great Bollin come to Landella? (*She turns to him and sings*) It is he. It is he! Hoist the flag of love!—Bollin. My heart's desire. Your handmaiden. She has yearned for thee. Spent her nights in madness. When will he come, oh when? The glorious one. The tower. The gate. To his Mimi.—And now he is here: Tall. Somber. Pale. Lonely. Sweet. Here!

(*She throws herself at his feet and tries to kiss his shoes.* BOLLIN *retreats*)

BOLLIN:

Be yourself. Anything that detracts from your dignity will force me to reconsider. I may turn back.

PRIMA DONNA:

Take pity on your troubled handmaiden.

BOLLIN:

You're not the first to see me coming.

PRIMA DONNA:

That's just it. All the great opera stars, Krauskopf and Höhmel, the unforgettable Graballi and the immortal Patzek, they've all, all seen him coming.

BOLLIN:

And none of them saw me leave.—What would you expect? Pull yourself together.—And who's this? An uninvited witness?

PRIMA DONNA:

This wretched camera boy? (*Stands up and drums on the photographer's back. Shamefacedly*) He's my fiancé.

BOLLIN:

That's your private affair.

PRIMA DONNA:

I'm ashamed of him.—It's finished, finished! Our engagement is broken. Go away, camera boy, this minute. (*She tries to push him out of the room.* BOLLIN *restrains them both*)

BOLLIN:

Just a minute, please. Your fiancé's paraphernalia suggest that he might be a photographer.

PRIMA DONNA:

Let the earth swallow me!

BOLLIN:

Have I guessed right? He takes pictures?

PRIMA DONNA:

I have to admit it.

BOLLIN:

Excellent. Let's put him to work, my dear. (*He pushes them both back into the room*) Why not? He will enrich my archives. Hm, postcard size will do. Why didn't I think of it before? A visual record of my work . . .

PRIMA DONNA:

Then you want him to stay?

BOLLIN:

He will manifest the simultaneity of action and documentation.—Does your fiancé do color photography, or only black and white?

PRIMA DONNA (*opens a portfolio*):

See for yourself.

BOLLIN:

Not unimpressive. But give me your opinion as a specialist. Don't you need a green filter to bring out the reds? (*The quaking photographer nods several times*) Very well: Bathtub. An assortment of toilet articles, you may choose them yourself.

PRIMA DONNA:

Shouldn't we have flowers?

BOLLIN:

If you like, but not too many. Afterwards we'll want

lingerie, negligently scattered.—All perfectly normal. (*The* PRIMA DONNA *hands him flacons and flowers.* BOLLIN *distributes them artistically*) And this would be the best vantage point for your fiancé.

PRIMA DONNA:

Get a move on, Bodo. Didn't you hear Mr. Bollin? (*She pushes him toward the bathtub*)

BOLLIN:

A little more to the left. That's it. And you, if you don't mind, put your clothes over there. Spread them out nicely. After all, we're trying to enlighten the public.

PRIMA DONNA:

Ah, at last it dawns on me. (*A trill*) All this is to be immortalized. Landella in the tub, the hot water turning red, her fire draining, her soul (*trill*), her silvery soul rising with the steam, lightly, effortlessly. And on the bathtub rim of this death he sits, he, Bollin. Looking on as my soul departs. He lives on.—And this camera boy— don't shake so, you fool! (*To* BOLLIN) He's going to ruin the pictures, I warn you.

BOLLIN:

Do try to quiet him, to get him back to normal. That shouldn't be hard for you. (*He opens a suitcase*)

PRIMA DONNA:

Can't you pull yourself together, Bodo? This is the opportunity of my life. Or think of yourself if that's the way you feel about it. You'll be the talk of the town. You'll be able to open up your own shop. I can see it all: Düsseldorf, Königsallee. Three big windows. Showcases in the lobby of the opera. More orders than you can fill. Everybody'll want to have his picture taken by the man who immortalized the great Bollin and the expiring Landella. Bodo! Stop that repulsive shaking. Didn't you hear Mr. Bollin: everything has to look normal, perfectly normal. All right. I take it back. We're still engaged, united unto death. Well, maybe not quite, because you have to go on living and run straight to the darkroom . . .

BOLLIN:

In that case shall we . . .

PRIMA DONNA:

But he's still shaking.

BOLLIN:

Perhaps, my dear, his deficient technique is just what the situation demands, better than lifeless perfection. I shouldn't be displeased if some of the pictures came out a little fuzzy or even lopsided.

PRIMA DONNA:

What! Landella lopsided!

BOLLIN:

But all we want is documentation. Who said anything about art?

PRIMA DONNA:

Landella refuses to be a blur. What have this insect's sick nerves to do with Landella?

BOLLIN:

We can be glad if the color comes out.

PRIMA DONNA:

And my expression? Do you want people to say that Landella had no expression in her last moments? What of the newspapers? My public?

BOLLIN:

They won't see a thing. You have my word for it.

PRIMA DONNA:

What! Such documents belong to the world. And you want them to gather dust in the drawer?—No, they will appear tomorrow. Blow them up big. Send three to Meier-Wellenberg, four to the *Mirror,* two for Stubbenrauch and one for the evening edition. And what would you think of an attractive little album, signed by yourself?

BOLLIN:

You overestimate my influence with the publishers.

PRIMA DONNA:

Don't make me laugh. If you just write a preface, they'll all come running.

BOLLIN:

I could claim author's rights. It's my idea, my investment . . .

PRIMA DONNA:

Of course. We'll split the royalties three ways. My share will go to the Fund for Aged and Impoverished Actors. I trust you to look out for my interests. Shouldn't we begin?

BOLLIN:

You took the words out of my mouth. Take your things off. I'll be running the bath. (*Loosens his tie, takes off his jacket, rolls up his shirtsleeves*)

PRIMA DONNA:

Weren't we speaking of a series, showing the development of the drama?—Why shouldn't we start with a friendly chat here on the divan?

BOLLIN:

I can do without. Get those rags off!

PRIMA DONNA:

You could be a little more gracious. How's my make-up? A little more rouge?

BOLLIN:

Fiddlesticks! There'll be plenty of color in a minute. (*Snaps open a knife*)

PRIMA DONNA:

Don't be crude, Bollin.

BOLLIN:

Forgive me.

PRIMA DONNA:

Don't mention it. (*She makes up at the mirror.* BOLLIN *fondles the knife and looks at the photographer*)

BOLLIN:

What's eating you, man? You're doing all right. You put a black rag over your head—hear nothing, see nothing— you press the button, and tomorrow the dough comes rolling in.

PRIMA DONNA:

Such a poltroon! It's ridiculous.

BOLLIN:

Don't worry, son. I'll make it quick. Ten, fifteen minutes and you'll be through—Now come along, angel, you're beautiful enough.

PRIMA DONNA:

Why are you men always in such a rush?

BOLLIN:

I have another item on my program.

PRIMA DONNA:

Really?!

BOLLIN:

The afternoon is young.

PRIMA DONNA:

A little dissipation?

BOLLIN:

It all depends.

PRIMA DONNA:

Who is the sweet young thing?

BOLLIN:

Sweet is saying too much.

PRIMA DONNA:

Well?

BOLLIN:

Whom would you expect? La Hetzberg.

PRIMA DONNA:

What!

F

BOLLIN:

Why not?

PRIMA DONNA:

That . . . that . . .

BOLLIN:

She's had a marvelous press lately.

PRIMA DONNA:

Don't make me laugh.

BOLLIN:

Stubbenrauch says her voice has gained in volume . . .

PRIMA DONNA:

How perfectly ridiculous!

BOLLIN:

. . . without losing any of its sweetness. A rising star, that's what he called her.

PRIMA DONNA:

Hetzberg? She's fifth-rate if you ask me. Only last year she was doing operettas somewhere in the sticks. Maybe she can get by on the radio. A little Wolf, a little Schubert. But on the stage?

BOLLIN:

The critics don't seem to see it that way. (*He pulls a sheaf of clippings from his coat pocket*) Here: Rich mature voice. Here: Unforgettable evening. Here . . .

PRIMA DONNA (*knocks the clippings out of his hand*):

I'm really surprised at you.—Did you hear that, Bodo? Don't send that Stubbenrauch anything.—You can't mean it. The same day, right after you've . . . before Landella's body is . . . You intend to . . . (*She throws herself on the divan and weeps hysterically.* BOLLIN *scratches himself in embarrassment*)

BOLLIN:

Pooh-pooh. Always these petty jealousies.

PRIMA DONNA:

The same afternoon . . .

BOLLIN:

Now you've done it. Look at your make-up.

PRIMA DONNA:

It will be the death of me.

BOLLIN:

And suppose I put my little visit off until tomorrow?

PRIMA DONNA:

Never! Never! That pop warbler, that two-bit crooner . . .

BOLLIN:

All right, calm down. I'll wait till her next opening night. If she messes up Isolde, I'll drop the whole project. Now are you happy? (*The* PRIMA DONNA *cries harder than ever.* BOLLIN *to the photographer*) Quick . . . Shoot. Maybe that'll help. (*Flash. The* PRIMA DONNA *jumps up, rushes at the photographer, and pounds his back with her fists*)

PRIMA DONNA:

Who gives the orders around here? You'll take pictures when I tell you to . . .

BOLLIN:

It was quite appealing.

PRIMA DONNA:

Landella is known for her control, her poise, her . . .

BOLLIN:

Maybe there's nothing on the plate.

PRIMA DONNA:

We'll see.—But won't you kindly sit down—no, wait. An idea came to me as I was making up: Why shouldn't Bollin immortalize himself here over the sofa with my lipstick? Would you mind?

BOLLIN:

Begging your pardon, my dear, isn't that rather juvenile? (*Takes the lipstick*) Wengendorf wanted me to write in her diary.

PRIMA DONNA:

I am not Wengendorf.

BOLLIN:

Well, here's what I wrote: The law of series demands to be lived.—Now then. Do you want something special? Or just my name?

PRIMA DONNA:

Write: Bollin has come to call on the great Landella. No, better make it the unique Landella.

BOLLIN (*writes*):

Unique with a *k*?

PRIMA DONNA (*radiant*):

With or without, it makes no difference. (*Trill*) Bollin— Landella.

BOLLIN (*taking his distance*):

I wouldn't exactly call it a work of art. (*Looking at his hands*) Stinking mess! Oh, I'm sorry. You don't mind if I wash my hands? (*He washes his hands under the bathtub faucet. The* PRIMA DONNA *puts a teakettle on the electric hotplate*)

PRIMA DONNA:

And I'll serve us some tea.—Come now, Mr. Bollin, you won't do that to me, will you?

BOLLIN:

Everything will take its normal course.

PRIMA DONNA:

But you'll cancel the visit to Hetzberg.

BOLLIN:

We'll leave that open if you don't mind.

PRIMA DONNA:

It would really be in bad taste.

BOLLIN:

But if the series requires it. Nevertheless, I repeat: We'll see.

PRIMA DONNA:

I'm afraid it would put me out of sorts.

BOLLIN:

You prima donnas are so temperamental.

PRIMA DONNA:

But it is distressing to be put on the same level as some-body else.

BOLLIN:

Pathological ambition. Megalomania.

PRIMA DONNA:

It seemed to me that you of all people would be sensitive to differences of quality. How can you compare a voice that's in demand at every festival with the tortured sing-song of a third-rate chorus girl? (BOLLIN *dries his hands and steps forward with the towel*)

BOLLIN:

I'm not so crazy about her myself. Perhaps I ought to fol-low my own inner voice instead of listening to the critics.

PRIMA DONNA:

That's a very sensible plan.

BOLLIN:

Hard to carry out in the present crisis of the opera.

PRIMA DONNA:

Crisis? Come, come. Look at me. Sooner or later real talent gains recognition. And heaven knows nobody did me any favors.

BOLLIN:

Ah? You have only yourself to thank?

PRIMA DONNA:

I began at the bottom of the ladder. I was a nobody until Felsner discovered me.

BOLLIN:

My word, so now Felsner gets all the credit. What a fool I've been! I always thought that my poor efforts had something to do with it.

PRIMA DONNA (*cooing*):

Oh, Bollinkins. You *are* a wicked one!—I solemnly confess that if some years ago the greathearted Bollin hadn't put a certain Probstfeld . . .

BOLLIN:

Poor Edeltraut . . .

PRIMA DONNA:

Yes, that was her first name.

BOLLIN:

. . . A fine voice.

PRIMA DONNA:

For certain roles.

BOLLIN:

She was said to be irreplaceable.

PRIMA DONNA:

An opinion that soon had to be modified.

BOLLIN:

When I dropped in, she said: Bollin, let's make it an occasion.

PRIMA DONNA:

Candlelight?

BOLLIN (*nods*):

And then she put on a record. And as I went about my work, her voice rose from the phonograph.

PRIMA DONNA:

Tristan, I presume.

BOLLIN:

The effect was stupendous. It gave me an eerie feeling.

PRIMA DONNA:

And she? Was she calm?

BOLLIN:

Calmly, as though stirred by gentle melancholy, she listened. When the record ran down, she whispered faintly: Turn it over, Bollin, turn it over. I put on the other side, but I doubt if she heard the end.

PRIMA DONNA (*moved*):

So that's how it was.

BOLLIN:

That's how it was. And that night you sang her part.

PRIMA DONNA (*gaily*):

Heavens, how excited I was! But everything came out fine. That was my first big success.

BOLLIN:

And who was responsible for it?

PRIMA DONNA:

You, master. You alone! (*She tries to embrace him.* BOLLIN *pushes her away*)

BOLLIN:

My dear lady, please in the future avoid all physical contact . . .

PRIMA DONNA:

But I only wanted to . . .

BOLLIN:

My motives have too often been impugned. I have my reputation to think of. I'm normal! Bollin is normal!

PRIMA DONNA (*dejectedly*):

Perhaps I ought to serve the tea before it gets cold.

BOLLIN:

Please do. (*He puts his jacket on, straightens his tie, and adjusts his posture. They sit down on the divan and drink tea with extreme formality*)

PRIMA DONNA:

Have you planned your summer vacation?

BOLLIN:

I've decided to take a walking trip in the Sauerland.

PRIMA DONNA:

I've been toying with a similar idea myself. Recently a colleague of mine was raving about Lapland. The only thing that makes me hesitate is the mosquitoes.

BOLLIN:

And really why go abroad? What I always say is: See Germany first.

PRIMA DONNA:

How right you are! It's just too silly. Next season we're touring Italy again.

BOLLIN:

The Taunus, Hunsrück, the Eifel: those are the places to explore . . . People make too much fuss about palms and oleanders . . . Our native pines . . .

PRIMA DONNA:

By the way, what brought you to opera?—Keep your eyes open, Bodo.

BOLLIN:

To your illustrious self, you mean?

PRIMA DONNA:

To music in general. Haven't you been specializing in our leading musicians?

BOLLIN:

I've been going to Bayreuth regularly now for the last three years. (*Flash*)

PRIMA DONNA:

An entrancing city.

BOLLIN:

In an entrancing region. Ah, Franconia, the Fichtel Mountains. I've explored every corner of them on my walking trips.—Conifers . . . You see, there are the spruces . . .

PRIMA DONNA:

I remember. Your forester period.

BOLLIN:

Well, that was in Brandenburg. But you're right in supposing that my walking trips began with my—alas, abortive!—forester series. From spruce to pine it's only . . .

PRIMA DONNA:

How fascinating! But now you must tell me how, when, and why you took your great leap—your divine leap!—to the opera.

BOLLIN:

I have to admit that chance had something to do with it. (*Flash*)

PRIMA DONNA:

Really, you, with all your rigorous planning! It doesn't seem possible.

BOLLIN:

The misbegotten child of reason must also have its say: I came to the theater by chance.

PRIMA DONNA:

Oh, do tell me about it.

BOLLIN:

After foresters I converted to barbers. That occupational group seemed to promise satisfactory results.

PRIMA DONNA:

Very interesting. But what of the theater?

BOLLIN:

Patience, my dear. Mr. Kühle was my last barber. The new light was born in his shop. This is what happened: (BOLLIN *stands up and performs*) I step in. (*Flash*) He's alone, because apparently his assistants, well anyway, he's alone. A haircut? A shampoo? No, thank you. Give me a shave. And when he's through, I put it to him point-blank: Well, Mr. Kühle, now it's my turn. He understands instantly. He takes off his barber's coat and lets me strap him in the chair. I hang out the sign: Temporarily closed, and lock the door. I test the razors. I'm just about to begin when he yells: Oh, oh! and starts moaning.

PRIMA DONNA:

But you hadn't even.

BOLLIN:

That's where chance stepped in. All of a sudden he has a toothache. You laugh, my dear. And indeed, the situation was not without its comic aspect. I tried everything imaginable. Cologne. Cold compresses. I gave him tobacco to chew. Nothing helped.—What could I do but send him off to the dentist?

PRIMA DONNA:

And the opera? When at last will the curtain rise?

BOLLIN:

I'm coming to that.—Just as he's leaving for the dentist's, he says: Bollin, I know you have a weakness for barbers. Take my ticket. Second row center. You'll enjoy it. There's a singing barber in it. I wish you a pleasant evening.— And that's how I came to the opera.

PRIMA DONNA:

Rossini! *The Barber of Seville (She sings)*

BOLLIN (*enthusiastic*):

Ah! Believe me. Käfliger was singing. And how he sang! (*Removes his jacket again, takes the pose of an opera singer and sings without words: "Largo al factotum della città . . ." The* PRIMA DONNA *jumps up.* BOLLIN *ends with bravura. Several flashes*)

PRIMA DONNA:

Magnificent. Thrilling. Bodo! Did you hear that? (BODO *applauds*) Do you know what you've got, Bollin? You've got a voice.—That's the plain and simple truth. From now on I shall think of you and speak to you as a fellow artist. Ah, Bollin, my sweet little Bollin! What power! What volume! It's more than talent. You have genius.

BOLLIN:

That's just what Käfliger said. I called on him that same evening, you know, right after the performance.

PRIMA DONNA:

It almost makes me jealous. Why did our good Hansi have to discover you instead of me? But I won't let you go. It will be a scandal if you don't carve out a career for yourself.

BOLLIN:

My reputation might stand in the way.

PRIMA DONNA:

Not at all. All you need is a stage name. Bruno de Pollo. Or Pollino? Yes, that's it! Pollino.

BOLLIN:

Not bad. Not bad at all. But even so, I fear complications. And I'd need lessons.

PRIMA DONNA:

I'll teach you free of charge.

BOLLIN:

And my series? . . . Weren't we going to . . . (*He points to the bathtub*)

PRIMA DONNA:

Silly boy. The bathtub won't run away.

BOLLIN:

But what will the public think? Won't they be disappointed?—One more disappointment.

PRIMA DONNA:

Who cares what they think as long as the two of us . . .

BOLLIN:

Won't they say that Bollin has abdicated?

PRIMA DONNA:

. . . Not if a new Bollin is there to serve them in the form of Pollino.

BOLLIN:

May I remind you of our agreement?

PRIMA DONNA:

My poor darling! (*Flash*)

BOLLIN:

No familiarities please! (*To* BODO) I forbid you.

PRIMA DONNA (*caresses him*):

He's only trying to further your career.

BOLLIN:

Take your hands off me!—Shall I give up everything?

PRIMA DONNA:

Oh, Pollino!

BOLLIN:

Knowledge acquired by the sweat of my brow: cross-word puzzles, Old Saxon Christian epic, Greek goddess of delusion . .

PRIMA DONNA:

That voice. That forehead. Those eyebrows.

BOLLIN:

Resin of a tropical tree. Female beast of burden. Completed action.

PRIMA DONNA:

Those pale temples. That magnificent nose.

BOLLIN:

And all I've learned from nature: It has a spreading root and can be put to very much the same uses as the pine.

PRIMA DONNA:

That neck, those shoulders. To hold them, to pine away, to . . .

BOLLIN:

But near the timber line grows the dwarf spruce, also known as miniature spruce . . .

PRIMA DONNA (*embraces him*):

My swan, my ambrosia . . .

BOLLIN:

No! I choose to be normal.

PRIMA DONNA:

Oh, my morning prayer . . .

BOLLIN:

I ought to be ashamed of myself . . .

PRIMA DONNA:

Yes, yes, shame, sin, vice . . .

BOLLIN:

For that reason the dwarf spruce, also known . . .

PRIMA DONNA:

Anything you say: fall, resurrection, another fall . . .

BOLLIN:

. . . as miniature spruce . . . No!

PRIMA DONNA:

Yes!

BOLLIN:

Bollin is and remains normal! (*He tears himself loose, hurls her to the floor, seizes his jacket, and exits, leaping through the screen*) Bollin is normal!

PRIMA DONNA (*lying on the floor*):

Pollino! Pollino! (*Sobs. After a brief pause raises her head*) Bodo! What do you think of this pose? Taken from a distance and not too foreshortened? (*The photographer steps back. Flash*) Maybe you'd better take another: Pollino! (*Flash*) And still another: Pollino! Pollino! (*Flash*)

CURTAIN

Act IV

Prologue

(BOLLIN *stands in front of the curtain. He has aged and is carelessly dressed. Beside him a phonograph. From the loudspeaker pours the aria from* Tannhäuser: *"To thee, goddess of love . . ." He lets the record run down, hums the melody, tries to sing, and gives up. He limps back and forth, takes folders out of the filing cabinet, which is larger than before, and puts them back*)

BOLLIN:

Gone! Gone!—Lord, to think of all I've learned—and still remember—partly. Monteverdi, Cesti, *Il Pomo d'oro*, 1666. Stradella, Scarlatti, Lully: from kitchen helper to court composer. Couperin, Rameau. Then the eighteenth century. Grand opera—comic opera. And if Gluck hadn't come along, who knows, who knows? Not to mention my special favorites: Mascagni, Leoncavallo, the so-called veristic opera. Puccini? Not bad, but so lyrical. *Tosca* can still get by. Who was it that sang Floria that time?—Hm. (*He shakes his head*) Gone! Gone!—And then my great period with Wagner. Time and time again he gave me new strength. When I was half crushed by work and responsibility, when I was ready to give up, yes, give up, it was his leitmotives that lifted me above the vexations of everyday life.

(*He strokes the phonograph records and tries again to sing*)

What's the use? It's all over.—Never will Bollin be a singer. Ah, the curtain calls. The wild waves of applause! —And now, with this stupid leg, there's no hope at all.

Has Bollin overreached himself? Has hobnobbing with
the art world destroyed his sense of innocent enjoyment,
his unreflecting normalcy, and sowed the seeds of megalomania in their place? Things have been going wrong ever
since you got the creative bug. First that appendix trouble
at the height of the season. Hardly out of the hospital
when a cop shoots you in the leg. Why? Because he mis-
takes Bollin for a thief, a common ordinary thief. All
right. The city has to pay up. But you'd hardly call it
unearned income.

(*He limps up and down*) Gone, gone.—Bollin ought to
start preparing for his old age. What does he know of old
age? Nothing.

(*The telephone rings*) Yes? Hi, Erwin. I sound sad? Maybe
so. It'll pass. A little slump, that's all. And what's
cooking with you? A big deal? That's what you always say; and the next day I read all about it in the
Mirror. Some servant girl or doctor's receptionist. I'm
against the death penalty, you know, but bunglers like
you, always in a hurry, may make me change my mind.—
What? Hm. Hm. That sounds better. What's her name?
A widow? But not under seventy? Hm. Good. Good.
Would I like to collaborate? You ought to know better.
I've never worked with anybody. And my Uncle Max
always said.—Too risky, Erwin, yes, risky. I've always
been a lone wolf. Hm. Hm. All right. I'll look her over.
But no promises. Will do. But be on time. Bollin doesn't
like to be kept waiting. (*He hangs up*)
Mrs. Toothsome. Colonel's widow. Eighty-three. A ripe
old age. A splendid age. A magnificent age. (*Exits*)

CURTAIN

Onkel, Onkel

(The outskirts of the city. An abandoned building site.
Piles of gravel, scaffolding. BOLLIN *is standing on a mortar*
pail. He looks expectantly in the direction of the city.
SPRAT *and* SLICK *approach slowly)*

SPRAT:
  Mister?

SLICK:
  Mister, aintcha got a thing?

SPRAT:
  Yeah, mister, give it here.

SLICK:
  Aintcha? Just one?

SPRAT:
  Hey, mister.

SLICK:
  You deaf?

BOLLIN:
  No!

SLICK:
  Only one, mister.

BOLLIN:
  I ain't got nothing.

SPRAT:
  Take a look. Maybe you got sumpin.

BOLLIN:
  Such as what?

SPRAT:
  Just a thing.

BOLLIN:
  What kind of a thing?

SPRAT:
  Everybody's got sumpin.

SLICK:

Why wouldn't you?

BOLLIN:

Take my word for it, kids, I haven't. Come around to-morrow or next week, maybe I'll have something, but not today.

SPRAT:

Don't be like that, mister. Take a good look.

SLICK:

Sure, take a look.

SPRAT:

Or if you won't, I . . .

BOLLIN:

Keep your paws to yourself. Beat it, go on home, your mother wants you.

SPRAT:

We just been. Okay, you look. There, in your pocket. You got sumpin, sure you got sumpin.

SLICK:

We seen it before, didn't we?

SPRAT:

I'll say. Sumpin round, kind of a round thing, kind of shiny.

BOLLIN:

That was my watch.

SLICK:

Whadda you think we been talking about the whole time? Didn't I say it was some kind of a thing?

BOLLIN:

Listen to that! It's not some kind of a thing, it's a real watch. Later, when you're grown-up . . .

SPRAT:

We got no time to wait. Come on, give it here, we only want to look at it.

SLICK:

Thass right. Only look at it a second.

SPRAT:

It's interesting.

SLICK:

We won't twist anything.

SPRAT:

I only wanna hold it up to my ear.

SLICK:

Just for a second, mister.

BOLLIN:

But God help you if. (*He gives* SPRAT *the watch*)

SLICK:

What's it sound like?

SPRAT:

You got to keep quiet.

SLICK:

Can you hear anything?

SPRAT:

A little.

SLICK:

Huh?

SPRAT:

It tickles kind of.

SLICK:

Where?

SPRAT:

All over.

SLICK:

Give it here! Say, this is super! (*He snatches the watch*)

SPRAT:

Say, mister, whatcha doing out here in this gravel? It belongs to us, didn't you know that?

BOLLIN:

No, I didn't. And now give me back my watch.

SPRAT:

You can't hang around here without permission.

BOLLIN:

All right, make it snappy.

SPRAT:

'Cause it's our gravel.

BOLLIN:

You can keep the gravel. But hurry up with that . . .

SPRAT:

You waiting for sumpin, mister?

BOLLIN:

I'm telling you for the last time, kid, give me that watch.

SLICK:

Aintcha got some other thing?

BOLLIN:

No. Hand it over.

SPRAT:

Dja hear that, he don't wanna.

SLICK:

I heard him before you were born.

SPRAT:

He wants to keep everything for himself.

SLICK:

He don't realize that other people want sumpin too.

SPRAT:

All he can do is stand around on other people's property . . .

BOLLIN:

Well, now what?

SLICK:

Well, now we'll blow. Thanks a lot. (*The children run around one of the piles of gravel with* BOLLIN, *slightly limping, after them*)

SPRAT *and* SLICK (*half singing*):

>   Mister, mister, aintcha got a thing,
>   Mister, just a little thing,
>   Any little thing.
>   Mister, mister, aintcha, aintcha,
>   Aintcha, aintcha, aintcha got
>   Any little dingus,
>   Hidden in your pocket.
>   Mister, mister, aintcha got a thing . . .

(*They exit*)

BOLLIN:

Hey, kids, don't run away. I didn't mean it. Damn gravel.
Got my shoes all full of it. And my leg. Now I see what
I'm up against. I always thought a little limp wouldn't
give me any trouble. And now this has to happen. It's
gone, I'll never see it again. It was only a cheap one, but
even so. You get attached to these things. It was Uncle
Max's. Who do those kids think they are? Our gravel!
It's our gravel! (*He climbs up on the pail again*) Still no
sign of him. It must be a quarter past. I specially told
him: Be on time, Erwin. Sure. And where is he? It's certainly a quarter past, or even later. But I knew it all along.
Too risky, I said, too risky, Erwin. I'm a lone wolf, I've
never worked with anybody. Only because it's an old
lady, that's the only reason. It must be half past—or pretty
near. (*He throws pebbles*) Thing, thing, aintcha, aintcha.
A thing they call it. If I didn't have this trouble with my
leg—but as it is?

(SPRAT *and* SLICK *enter slowly from the left*)

SPRAT:

Mister.

BOLLIN:

There they are again. Well, give it here.

SPRAT:

Whatcha throwing at, mister?

BOLLIN:

Come on, give me that watch.

SPRAT:

He's messing up all the nice gravel.

SLICK:

He's bored, that's his trouble.

SPRAT:

You can't go chucking our gravel around, mister. Spose
we started throwing things that don't belong to us?

BOLLIN:

Where's my watch?

SLICK:

The thing? We ain't got it no more.

BOLLIN:

Then where is it?

SPRAT:

What, mister?

BOLLIN:

My watch, damn it. Or I'll beat the stuffings out of you.

SLICK:

You can try, mister. We'll run real slow.

BOLLIN:

What have you done with the watch, children?

SLICK:

He means the thing.

BOLLIN:

Okay, where is it?

SPRAT:

You married, mister?

BOLLIN:

No.—Say, you kids, what are your names?

SPRAT:

They call me Sprat. Does that interest you?

BOLLIN:

And him?

SLICK:

What kind of a game is this? Asking stupid questions.

SPRAT:

Hm.—Okay, then we'll play something else. Say, mister, you interested in women? I got a sister, she's got hair here under her arms.

BOLLIN:

Now see here, Sprat. You're a sensible little girl. Come over here. A little closer.

SLICK:

Watch out, Sprat, he's up to sumpin.

SPRAT:

I'm a minor, mister,

SLICK:

Good for a couple of years.

BOLLIN:

Now, children, don't get me wrong.

SPRAT:

Aintcha got another thing?

BOLLIN:

Come closer first, both of you.

SLICK:

Careful, Sprat, he wants to feel you up.

SPRAT (*takes a few steps*):

Take a look, mister. See if you ain't got sumpin someplace. Then we'll tell you what time it is. Won't we, Slick?

SLICK:

Sure.

SPRAT:

You think we can't read the thing? I learned when I was six, in first grade.

BOLLIN:

Really? Well, what time is it?

SPRAT:

Gimme the thing first. Up there, the black thing.

BOLLIN:

This? What you won't think of next! It's my fountain pen.
A present from my Uncle Max. I need it.

SPRAT:

What for?

BOLLIN:

To write letters.

SPRAT:

What kind of letters?

BOLLIN:

You wouldn't understand. I'll tell you later.

SPRAT:

Love letters, all full of smut?

SLICK:

Don't ask so many questions. Tell him to give us the
thing.

SPRAT:

Wait awhile. I'll get it.—Wanna know how old I am?

BOLLIN:

All I want is my watch.

SPRAT:

Don't be like that, mister. You ain't really like that.
What kind of letters do you write? You said you'd tell us
later. It's later now.

BOLLIN:

Business letters and so on.

SPRAT:

What do you mean, and so on?

BOLLIN:

Well, other kinds. Come on, give me my watch. I'm getting good and sick of this.

SPRAT:

You know what you are? You're a spoilsport.

SLICK:

Whyn't you ask him how babies are made?

SPRAT:

He wants me to ask you how babies are made.

BOLLIN:

Nonsense!

SPRAT:

Well, how are they made?

BOLLIN:

That's not so easy to explain.

SPRAT:

You could try.

BOLLIN:

Well, haven't you ever heard about the stork?

SLICK:

Nuts! Either you give the thing here or I'll chuck your watch in the sewer. (*He bends down*)

BOLLIN:

That won't do you any good. My Uncle Max.

SLICK:

Don't you take another step or I'll open my hand.

BOLLIN:

It's a keepsake. Please, children.

SPRAT:

Didn't you hear him, mister? He'll chuck it in the sewer if you don't.

SLICK:

I've chucked better things than that.

SPRAT:

You got to give us the thing. We only want to look at it.

SLICK:

I'll count to three: one, two, two and a half . . .

BOLLIN:

But give it back! (*Gives* SPRAT *his fountain pen*)

SLICK:

Looks pretty nifty close up. I didn't think so from over here.

SPRAT:

I could use it.

SLICK:

What for?

SPRAT:

Oh, just . . . I got things to write too sometimes.

BOLLIN:

Well, how about it?

SLICK:

Take it easy.

SPRAT:

You ain't nice, mister. You always want everything right away. Whatcha waiting for anyway? This is our gravel, didn't I tell you before?

BOLLIN:

How about it, I said.

SLICK:

Come on, let's beat it. There's nothing doing around here.

SPRAT:

Was your Uncle Max nice?

SLICK:

Don't ask such personal questions.

SPRAT:

Well, good-by, mister.

BOLLIN:

But you promised . . .

SPRAT:

Go on, tell him what time it is.

SLICK:

All right. It's exactly about a quarter of two.

BOLLIN:

You stay right here! My watch! My fountain pen! (BOLLIN *limps around the pile of gravel after the children*)

SLICK *and* SPRAT:

> Mister, mister, aintcha got a thing,
> Mister, just a little thing,
> Any little thing.
> Mister, mister, aintcha, aintcha,
> Aintcha, aintcha, aintcha got
> Any little dingus
> Hidden in your pocket.
> Mister, mister . . .

(Both exit)

BOLLIN:

What did the little creep say? A quarter of two. Can that be right? It certainly can't be much less. Maybe I'd better go home, or maybe I could try it alone. Suppose I write him a note and fasten it on here. Up high, so the kids can't get it. Say! Paper? Sure, all I need. Backing? No problem. Hell! My fountain pen. As true as my name's Bollin, I'm heading for trouble. Never again. Calls me up five times a week. Wouldn't there be some little job? And take me with you, and I'm your man. You can count on me.—Sure. And does he show up? Erwin! Erwin! Maybe he'll still come. (*He throws some more pebbles*) Or I'll do it alone. It really does bother me.—I wouldn't have thought so. But that's the way it goes.—I never had such a. Should I try it alone?

(SLICK *and* SPRAT *enter slowly from the left*)

SPRAT:

There he goes. Throwing our gravel again.

BOLLIN:

You still got my things?

SPRAT:

You got your nerve, mister.

BOLLIN:

Give me my things.

SLICK:

What things?

BOLLIN:

My watch and my fountain pen.

SLICK:

Oh! We still gottem, ain't we, Sprat?

SPRAT:

Sure. We still gottem.

BOLLIN (*helplessly*):

Couldn't you return them?

SLICK:

Naw.

BOLLIN:

Why not?

SPRAT:

You're on our gravel.

SLICK:

Mister! Say, whatcha got in your pocket?

BOLLIN:

Here? Nothing.

SLICK:

No, the other one.

SPRAT:

That big bulge.

SLICK:

Looks like sumpin big and heavy.

BOLLIN:

Where's my watch?

SPRAT:

You always got that in there, mister?

SLICK:

What kind of a thing is that? Sumpin special?

BOLLIN:

Anyway, it's not for children.

SPRAT:

Aw, don't be like that, mister.

SLICK:

Give us a look, from over here.

BOLLIN:

No!

SPRAT:

You can feel me up. Wherever you please. I won't yell.

BOLLIN:

Forget it. I said no.

SPRAT:

Or do you like boys better?

BOLLIN:

That's enough of that. Give me my watch.

SLICK:

If you won't, you won't. Guess it's just some old thing. Say, let's blow.

BOLLIN:

You stay right here. Give me my watch and fountain pen right away, or . . . or . . .

SPRAT:

Or what?

SLICK:

I'll say: Show us the thing or we'll clear out.

SPRAT:

It don't matter. Come on.

BOLLIN:

Here! (*Takes his revolver out of his pocket*)

SLICK:

What kind of a thing is that?

BOLLIN:

A revolver.

SPRAT:

Let's touch it.

BOLLIN:

Certainly not.

SPRAT:

I wanna touch it.

BOLLIN:

No!

SPRAT:

Just feel it once.

SLICK:

So that's a revolver.

BOLLIN:

And now give me my watch, or . . . (*He aims at* SPRAT)

SPRAT (*laughs*):

Look, he's trying to scare us with his thing.

BOLLIN:

It's got two bullets in it.

SLICK:

Hell, that's what I thought in the first place. Either it's a revolver, or it's sumpin else.

BOLLIN:

See here, children, if I pull the trigger . . .

SPRAT:

Just touch it. (BOLLIN *lowers the revolver*)

BOLLIN:

No, no, and no. That's enough now. Give me my watch.

SPRAT:

Only with two fingers.

BOLLIN:

It's really not for children. Believe me, it's dangerous. There's going to be trouble.

SLICK:

Anybody can say that. I bet it's only a fifty-cent water pistol or even cheaper.

SPRAT:

Or a mickyscope.

SLICK:

Don't be silly, they look different. Bet it's a water pistol. Must be. If it was a revolver, he'd shoot.

SPRAT:

Just the same I'd like to know . . .

SLICK:

Ask him.

SPRAT:

Mister?— (BOLLIN *stands there thoughtful and absent*) Sumpin wrong?

BOLLIN (*with a start*):

What?—Come on now, my watch and my fountain pen. Hand them over, I need them. It's my watch and my fountain pen. My Uncle Max gave it to me when, the fountain pen too.

SLICK:

We heard that a year ago. You said that before.

SPRAT:

We're talking about something entirely different.

SLICK:

About that dingus you got in your hand—yeah, that's right! (BOLLIN *looks absently at his revolver, unsure of himself*)

SPRAT:

I wanna touch it.

SLICK:

Don't be like that, mister. If she wants to so bad. Besides, it's her birthday today if you really wanna know.

SPRAT:

Right. It's my birthday.

BOLLIN (*hesitantly*):

But I'm telling you! (*Hands* SPRAT *the revolver*)

SPRAT:

Feels cold. Like a toad. Wonder if it croaks when you squeeze it.

BOLLIN:

All right now, give it back.

SPRAT:

It's real nice, eh, Slick?

SLICK:

Boy, oh boy!

SPRAT:

Wouldn't you like to?

SLICK:

Yeah, that would be sumpin.

SPRAT:

Whatcha do with the thing, mister?

BOLLIN:

Nothing. I just happen to have it.

SPRAT:

I don't believe you. Whatcha do with it?

SLICK:

Anybody knows that, Sprat. He's got it for protection.

SPRAT:

And if you squeeze this here?

BOLLIN:

Watch out, it's loaded.

SLICK:

He's trying to scare us again.

SPRAT:

Natch.

BOLLIN:

Good God—Erwin!

SPRAT:

He's scared.

SLICK:

Erwin don't exist.

SPRAT:

Or Uncle Max neither.

BOLLIN:

Are you crazy, drop that thing, come on, drop it, drop it!

SPRAT:

See, he calls it a thing too. And he was trying to tell us it's a revolver. (*She shoots,* BOLLIN *falls to the ground*)

SPRAT:

Look. His eyes are all white.

SLICK:

This is crazy.

SPRAT:

Come on, let's blow. What was he doing here anyway, when it's our gravel?—And what'll we do with the thing?

SLICK:

It's a revolver. Didn't you hear?

SPRAT:

You know what we'll do?—Eek!

SLICK:

We could hang it on the wall. It'll look good.

SPRAT:

I got a different idea. You take it and threaten me.

SLICK:

And then?

SPRAT:

Then I beg for mercy and undo my braids.

SLICK:

What for?

SPRAT:

You gotta when you beg somebody for mercy.

SLICK:

Hm. And then?

SPRAT:

Then you gotta rape me.

SLICK:

Are you nuts?

SPRAT:

Sure, I read it in the paper. Conductor rapes minor.

SLICK:

Then I'll be the conductor. Hm? Howdya do it?

SPRAT:

Wait a second. Like this. (*She whispers in* SLICK's *ear*)

SLICK:

Where?

SPRAT:

Here where the thing is. The little round thing. (*She taps on her belly button*)

SLICK:

And then what happens?

SPRAT:

Then I get a baby, naturally.

SLICK:

Say, you're getting me all mixed up. And what about me?

SPRAT:

You? You'll be the father. Who else? Him?—Sure, and then we'll get married.

SLICK:

Why?

SPRAT:

'Cause that's the way it is. Come on, let's go. After the signpost, we run. Me first, then you. To the barn. That's where we'll do it.

SLICK:

That business with the conductor. I don't believe it.

SPRAT:

You think it's some different way? We can try.

SLICK:

Sure. We got plenty of time.

SPRAT *and* SLICK (*exit hopping. Half singing*):

      Mister, mister, aintcha, aintcha,

G

Aintcha, aintcha, aintcha got
Any little dingus
Hidden in your pocket.
(*Softly*) Mister, mister . . .

CURTAIN

Only Ten Minutes to Buffalo

A Play in One Act

Translated by Ralph Manheim

Cast of Characters

KRUDEWIL, an engineer

PEMPELFORT, a fireman

AXEL, a cowherd

KOTSCHENREUTHER, a painter

FRIGATE, a lady

(In the center of the stage a rusty old locomotive and tender, overgrown with moss. KRUDEWIL *at the window of the cab,* PEMPELFORT *on the tender. They look ahead with an air of moving at high speed.*

Green landscape with cows in the background.

In the left foreground the painter KOTSCHENREUTHER *is sitting at his easel, working on a picture.* AXEL *in farm clothes is looking on)*

AXEL:

It's beginning to look like a ship.

KOTSCHENREUTHER:

Exactly.—A frigate.

AXEL:

Oh, don't mind me. We farmers don't get to see those things very often.

KOTSCHENREUTHER:

You've got something on your mind, Axel. Out with it.

AXEL:

Well, you see. A famous painter like you. I don't get it. Every morning you come out here, you look at the cows, you take measurements as if you knew something about cattle and were thinking of buying a heifer, and then . . . And then . . .

KOTSCHENREUTHER:

Then?

AXEL:

Then you make a ship out of it.

KOTSCHENREUTHER:

A frigate.

AXEL:

Well, anyway a sailboat.

KOTSCHENREUTHER (*stands up, compares his picture with the landscape*):

You've got to attune yourself to the new spirit. You've got to dive down under the old values . . . Then you'll discover new aspects, sensitive instruments, prophetic mechanisms, a virgin continent . . . and first of all you've got to throw all these stupid titles overboard. Cow, ship, painter, buttercup. They're all delusions, hallucinations, complexes. Do you think your cow minds if you call it a sailboat . . . or even a steamer?

AXEL:

You may be right. But what about my eyes? When I look and see—here a cow and there a ship . . .

KOTSCHENREUTHER:

That's just it, that's the big mistake. You look at things with your intellect. Keep your simplicity, start all over again from scratch. In the beginning was the ship. Later it developed into a cow, and the cow into a chess set, then the pyramids were built, then came journalism and with it the railroad—who knows what will happen tomorrow. —Bring me some sail juice, I'm thirsty.

AXEL:

You mean milk, sir?

KOTSCHENREUTHER:

Call it whatever you like, as long as it's as white as Moby Dick.

(AXEL *exits, the painter sits down and works intensely.* KRUDEWIL *opens the throttle wide. The locomotive howls plaintively*)

PEMPELFORT:

You'll have to go easier on the coal, it's not going to hold out very long.

KRUDEWIL:

I can always burn you.

PEMPELFORT:

Oh, you wouldn't do that!

KRUDEWIL:

You think I'm joking? I'll cut you up into neat little pieces and put them out in the air to dry. Then I'll shovel you in. (*He laughs loudly*)

PEMPELFORT:

For God's sake, don't grind your teeth like that—and slow down. Really we've got to go easy on fuel.

KRUDEWIL (*leans out the window in a rage*):

Who's running this engine, you or me?

PEMPELFORT:

The line's in bad shape around here. Really we've got to take on fuel. Oh, please believe me.

KRUDEWIL:

Nonsense. (*He speeds up*)

PEMPELFORT:

The last shovelful. (*Pleading*) Krudewil, Krudewil.

KRUDEWIL:

Pull yourself together, Pempelfort, I warn you. I won't stand for it.—Ha, in thirty minutes we'll be in Buffalo, then all our misery will be over. Bells will be rung, street lamps will be smashed . . .

PEMPELFORT:

I beg you on bended knee.

KRUDEWIL:

Shirts will be changed and breasts anointed . . .

PFMPELFORT:

Oh, if you'd only listen.

KRUDEWIL:

. . . nails will be cut and kneecaps oiled. There will be laughter, do you hear me, laughter.

PEMPELFORT:

I'm so glad, really I am. But if we could only stop for three minutes. It's such a lovely spot, it would be a sin not to stop. The cows are so friendly. They're just asking to help us. (KRUDEWIL *pulls the brake and leans out the window*)

KRUDEWIL:

But not one second more. (PEMPELFORT *jumps down off the tender and collects cow flop with a shovel*) What an awful place. That smell of butter. It'll give me jaundice.

PEMPELFORT:

Don't be unkind. They're our providers.

KRUDEWIL:

I'm sure we'd have made it.

PEMPELFORT:

Never.—I'm not trying to teach you your business. I know you're the engineer. When it comes to running the engine, you're tops. But I know a few things too. I'm somebody too.

KRUDEWIL (*contemptuously*):

Sure, you're the fireman.

PEMPELFORT:

That's right, the fireman. And my eye tells me whether we've got enough and for how long and when and whether we've got to take on fuel.

KRUDEWIL:

You're probably right. You are a first-class fireman. But get going. We're falling behind schedule.

PEMPELFORT:

Just this one and that one over there. Dry as tinder. (*He approaches the painter*) You a painter?

KOTSCHENREUTHER (*irritably*):

Don't bother me. Come around some other time. I'm busy with the rigging.

KRUDEWIL:

Come along, Pempelfort, leave the man alone. You've still got the bolts to do.

PEMPELFORT:

Yes, that's a fact. Here I come. (*He hammers at the bolts,* KRUDEWIL *blows a signal and starts up*)

KRUDEWIL:

Partenza!

PEMPELFORT:

Stop, stop. Wait for me. (*He runs, marking time, beside the engine, stumbles, falls, jumps on, sits breathless on the tender.* KRUDEWIL *laughs*) You shouldn't do that. You know how nervous I am. I can't stand to be frightened like that. I do my best, don't I? We've been under steam for five days now. And you have me to thank for it, me and nobody else.

KRUDEWIL:

That's the truth, Pempelfort, you've worked hard.

PEMPELFORT:

Anyway, I'd much rather have stayed on the ship. What a lovely ship and always plenty of fresh air. But you had to mutiny and clear out.

KRUDEWIL:

You could have stayed on. Scrubbing decks, eating hardtack, sleeping before the mast—forget it. This landscape doesn't appeal to me at all. Look at all those cows.

PEMPELFORT:

You've got something there. The livestock is indeed abundant. I wonder who milks them all?

KRUDEWIL:

What do we care? We have our goal, and its name is Buffalo, and when we get there you'll see a thing or two.

PEMPELFORT:

For instance?

KRUDEWIL:

You're always asking questions. That's where they cook with gas. Anchors aweigh and decks cleared for action. Ahoy! Ahoy! (*He utters a terrifying laugh*)

PEMPELFORT:

It frightens me when you laugh like that. You're plotting something.

KRUDEWIL:

That's for sure.

PEMPELFORT:

Something bad?

KRUDEWIL:

It depends on how you look at it.

PEMPELFORT:

Tell me the truth. I couldn't stand it for you to go off the deep end again just as we're coming to the end of our long journey.—We shouldn't have done it, leaving her flat like that.

KRUDEWIL:

Who wants a woman for a captain . . .

PEMPELFORT:

Commander.

KRUDEWIL:

Admiral for my money. Anyway it's unbearable. A woman's place is in bed, or in a rocking chair knitting. (*He laughs*)

PEMPELFORT:

Don't laugh, or . . .

KRUDEWIL:

Or what?

PEMPELFORT:

Or I'll leave you.

KRUDEWIL:

You leave *me*?

PEMPELFORT:

That's right.

KRUDEWIL:

Just a minute. (*He reads the speed gauge*) We're doing a good ninety whatyoumaycallits. Reckon that up in knots and tell me . . .

PEMPELFORT:

I don't care. If you're plotting something wicked, I can't be your friend any more. But if you promise me that when we get there you'll go to bed early—it's only reasonable after such an exhausting trip . . .

KRUDEWIL:

Stow it. Not another word.

PEMPELFORT:

Then I'll have to do it. (*He rises and climbs up on the edge of the tender*)

KRUDEWIL:

Sit down, man. He's out of his mind.

PEMPELFORT:

Oh no. Pempelfort's sane, perfectly sane. I've seen through you and I can guess how you'll end up. You're going to commit some crime, there'll be blood on your hands. You give me the creeps, Krudewil. (*He starts to jump off the tender.* KRUDEWIL *climbs quickly out of the cab and grabs him. They wrestle, fall off the tender, run after it, jump on, go on wrestling; the engine spurts steam, howls. The painter jumps up, takes paper and charcoal*)

KOTSCHENREUTHER:

Ha, what do I see! Jacob wrestling with the angel. Quick, a sketch. Nobody ever saw that, nobody ever got that down on paper, it's alive, it's timely and yet timeless. That's got to be in my picture, transcendence between foremast and mainmast, in the teeth of the nor'wester. Catch as catch can, Jacob wrestling with the angel. (*He sits down and paints.* KRUDEWIL *has overpowered* PEMPELFORT)

KRUDEWIL:

Are you going to try that again? Leaving your best friend in the lurch?

PEMPELFORT:

Only if you promise me. Swear it. Swear (KRUDEWIL *raises his right hand*) you'll never leave me alone again.

KRUDEWIL:

By the speed of our engine. (*They stand facing into the wind*)

PEMPELFORT:

Swear you'll go to bed as soon as we pull in.

KRUDEWIL:

By the roadbed between here and Buffalo.

PEMPELFORT:

Swear you'll say your evening prayers.

KRUDEWIL:

By the God who works the switches.

PEMPELFORT:

Swear you'll never, never again go to that accursed dive with those people.

KRUDEWIL:

But they're perfectly harmless. (*He begins to let his hand fall*)

PEMPELFORT:

Go on. That you'll never again set foot in that dive.

KRUDEWIL:

By every joint in the rails and every milestone, by every swallow and telegraph pole (*he points ahead*)—by all the impenetrable signals . . . Damn it, the signal's up. (*He hurries to the cab and throws on the brake*) That could have ended bad. Oh well, lucky again. I'll never do that again, not at that speed.

PEMPELFORT:

An oath is an oath, my boy, now you're at anchor.

KRUDEWIL:

Will you please stop using those nautical terms. Anyway, knock those bolts in.

PEMPELFORT:

I just did a minute ago.

KRUDEWIL:

Step on it.

PEMPELFORT:

Okay, if you insist. (*He climbs down with a hammer and hammers at the wheels*) But you won't just start up again and make me run after you. Do you hear me, Krudewil?

KRUDEWIL:

I'll drop you a card to notify you.

PEMPELFORT:

Go on, make jokes. One day when I have ceased to be, you'll realize whom you've abused and tormented. Then you'll be sorry, but too late, Krudewil, too late.

KRUDEWIL (PEMPELFORT *is picking flowers*):

Poor fellow, you must be mighty unhappy with nothing but flowers to comfort you and maybe a bedraggled butterfly. Only fifteen minutes to Buffalo, then you can strew flowers all over the station and give the stationmaster a bunch of dandelions. (*He lights up his pipe. Picking flowers*, PEMPELFORT *approaches* KOTSCHENREUTHER)

PEMPELFORT (*amazed*):

My goodness. Another painter!

KOTSCHENREUTHER (*sullenly*):

What do you mean, another?

PEMPELFORT:

Less than ten minutes ago we had to stop in the open fields because we were out of fuel, and whom do you suppose I saw?

KOTSCHENREUTHER:

Joan of Arc, I suppose.

PEMPELFORT:

Wrong. There was a field exactly like this, and somebody was sitting there painting.

KOTSCHENREUTHER (*jumps up*):

Don't talk nonsense. What was the fellow painting? Probably flowers or butterflies.

PEMPELFORT:

That's just it. He was in a very bad humor. He wouldn't let me look at his picture. And I wanted so much to see it.

KOTSCHENREUTHER:

Hm. Large format? And what about his palette?

PEMPELFORT:

Blue, lots of blue. He was working very hard. He said he was just about to do the rigging. Maybe he did seascapes.

KOTSCHENREUTHER:

Just as I thought. Drellmann, that ridiculous imitator. Well, my boy, you just wait, I'll wash your brush out. (*He packs up picture, easel, and paints*) Stealing my ideas. Probably the wrestling match too. That provincial bigshot. Never even heard of the avant-garde. My friend, my name is Kotschenreuther. Remember that name. I am a man whose watch is several centuries fast. Anyone who makes an appointment with me is sure to be late. (*Heavily laden, he exits left.* PEMPELFORT *stands there in amazement, but has to run because* KRUDEWIL *is starting off*)

KRUDEWIL:

All aboard! *Partenza!* (PEMPELFORT *jumps on*)

PEMPELFORT:

I can't stand it any more.

KRUDEWIL:

Oh hell, firemen have to put up with these things. We'll be there soon. Then you'll have time to whine and bellyache.—Give her a few shovelfuls.

PEMPELFORT (*shovels fuel into the fire*):

I'll never believe you again. Not a single word. You're a scoundrel, that's what you are. You promised, you swore by all the open grade crossings in the world. But I know the lay of the land: as soon as we get there, I'll be alone again. I'll be so scared I'll have to lock all the doors.

KRUDEWIL:

You're talking a lot of nonsense. Laugh, man, laugh. Isn't this the life? Safe on the rails. No swell, no reefs, no scurvy, no Davy Jones. Always straight ahead, today in Dallas, tomorrow in Buffalo—if this landscape could only think of some other way to look. Desert for all I care, sand, sand, sand, with nothing on it but a few empty tin cans to port and starboard. As long as there's no more cows and no more daisies. (PEMPELFORT *smells his flowers*)

PEMPELFORT:

You have no feeling for nature.

KRUDEWIL:

I need variety.

PEMPELFORT:

Yes, I know all about that. Vice, filth, drunkenness, shameful situations, low passions, froth, curses, disgust, obscene pleasures, and no repentance.

KRUDEWIL:

What else have I got? An engineer has nobody but himself to fall back on.

PEMPELFORT:

Ridiculous excuses. Anyway you've never driven a passenger train. Only freight trains.

KRUDEWIL (*declaiming*):

The freight train, the freight train. It's longer than a passenger train. How about it?

PEMPELFORT:

You're only trying to change the subject.

KRUDEWIL:

Aw please. Only three verses.

PEMPELFORT:

No.

KRUDEWIL:

I'll begin. (*He climbs up on the roof of the locomotive*)

PEMPELFORT:

If it were only a chantey, and we could weigh anchor.

KRUDEWIL:

They blow each other's candles out
And spit in one another's stout.
Each one calls the other crummy.
And all together cheat at rummy.
Their ignorance is quite prodigious,
But over it their gall builds bridges,
And on the bridges clanks and rumbles
The freight train, the freight train.

PEMPELFORT (*gesticulating on the tender*):

They're always full of bright suggestions
And conversation never lags.
With tact and poise and velvet paw
They beat each other to the draw
And rip each other's views to rags.
The freight train, the freight train.

KRUDEWIL (*straddling the locomotive*):

They give each other helping hands,
A gentleman can do no less.
They have a big cast-iron safe
To safeguard inner emptiness.
Each one claims the other's sick.
They proudly on the platform stand,
Waving handkerchief and hand.
The freight train, the freight train.

PEMPELFORT (*jumps down, runs alongside the locomotive, jumps back on again*):

An omnibus, an omnibus

Is filled with tedium and worry.
The bus outruns the river,
The river isn't in a hurry.
The winner's always miles ahead,
They filch each other's daily bread.
They guzzle beer both dark and light.
An angry beast howls in the night.
The freight train, the freight train . . .

KRUDEWIL:

. . . is longer than a passenger train.

(*He laughs, blows the whistle, suddenly pulls the brake*)
Curses!

PEMPELFORT:

What's the matter? What are you stopping for?

KRUDEWIL:

There's somebody lying there.

PEMPELFORT:

Where? (*They both look out the cab window*)

KRUDEWIL:

On the tracks.

PEMPELFORT:

Oh my! Maybe they're bound, unconscious, gagged, breathing their last gasp.

KRUDEWIL:

Dangerous place around here. All those cows are just camouflage. Go on. Go take a look.

PEMPELFORT:

Me?

KRUDEWIL:

Who else?

PEMPELFORT:

But, but . . .

KRUDEWIL:

Go on, step on it. Or I suppose you'd like to send the engineer?

PEMPELFORT:

But suppose something moves. Suppose they come.

KRUDEWIL (*draws a pistol*):

Here, I brought this with me. What would the captain need a gun for?

PEMPELFORT:

She's probably missed it.

KRUDEWIL:

Who cares? We can make good use of it now. Get going, I'll cover you. (PEMPELFORT *exits*) Those cows are up to no good. It would be safer to knock the whole lot of them off. We could do it now. Or later on the wing. (PEMPELFORT *comes back*)

PEMPELFORT:

Krudewil.

KRUDEWIL:

Back so soon?

PEMPELFORT:

It's a woman.

KRUDEWIL:

Pretty?

PEMPELFORT:

Stop fiddling with that gun.

KRUDEWIL:

I asked you if she was pretty.

PEMPELFORT:

I don't know, I didn't get close enough . . .

KRUDEWIL:

Go take a good look.

PEMPELFORT:

Wouldn't you rather go? You know more about these things.

KRUDEWIL:

Get moving. (*He raises the pistol menacingly.* PEMPELFORT

exits) He's scared of a woman. He trembles at the sight of a cotton, wool, or silk skirt chock-full of woman. (PEMPELFORT *comes back*) Good God, man, you look like a ghost. Did she bite you or pull your shirttails? (*He laughs, then breaks off, suspecting something*) Hey, Pempelfort, stop rattling your teeth. Pull yourself together.

PEMPELFORT:

It's her.

KRUDEWIL:

My God! Frigate?

PEMPELFORT:

She looks mighty angry.

KRUDEWIL:

In uniform?

PEMPELFORT:

Flags on every mast. And besides she's smoking cigars.

KRUDEWIL:

Two?

PEMPELFORT:

Three. By turns.

KRUDEWIL:

Maybe she's not sore at us.

PEMPELFORT:

You don't know her.

KRUDEWIL:

Did she see you?

PEMPELFORT:

I don't think so.

KRUDEWIL:

Hm. I've got a little idea.

PEMPELFORT:

Krudewil, you're not thinking of . . .

KRUDEWIL:

Why not? Couldn't the visibility have been bad? Ground fog, night, snow flurries.

PEMPELFORT:

Krudewil.

KRUDEWIL:

What's the matter? Ordinarily I wouldn't even have been able to stop.

PEMPELFORT:

But you did.

KRUDEWIL:

It was careless of me. Come on. Off we go. (*He climbs into the cab.* PEMPELFORT *stands between the rails with arms outstretched*) For the Lord's sake, Pempelfort. Just three minutes more. I can already see a dim layer of haze, Buffalo, freedom. (*He resigns himself*) All right, untie her.

PEMPELFORT:

She's not tied. She's just sitting there with her legs crossed. She's made herself comfortable. She looks terrifying. Terrifying. I'm going to beg her forgiveness. (*Exits*)

KRUDEWIL:

It's her all right. No doubt about it.—The gun! What'll I do with it? Here? No. Here? That's no good either. I'll put it in the tender or up on the roof. (*He climbs up on the roof*) Here in the smokestack. (*He puts the pistol in the smokestack*) I can see it all. She'll want to put out to sea right this minute. God knows what kind of cargo she's taken on. We'll be a hundred days without sighting land. No more tracks, no more swallows, no telegraph poles, no more friendly stationmasters to welcome us. Nothing. A tipsy horizon, half-crazed gulls, and now and then a lighthouse. (*He climbs slowly down from the engine.* PEMPELFORT *comes back breathless*)

PEMPELFORT:

Course southeast. She's taken on pepper.

KRUDEWIL:

What else? Sticky weather? (*A bosun's whistle is heard*)

PEMPELFORT:

She clouted me one. And the flowers, I tried to give them to her, friendly like, and she ate them. Stems and all.

KRUDEWIL:

Oh, if only ground fog or snow flurries had cut off the view. She's tacking and turning like a school ship: spick and span, solemn, visits allowed only on Sunday.

PEMPELFORT:

She's got the wind up and she's going to ask questions. We'd better bone up. From flying jib to spanker?

KRUDEWIL:

Mizzenmast, mainmast, and foremast. Mizzen staysail, mizzen-topmast staysail, mizzen-topgallant staysail . . . mizzen-royal staysail . . .

PEMPELFORT:

Upper mizzen topsail, mizzen-topgallant sail, mizzen sky-sail. And now the mainmast: mainsail, lower main topsail, upper main topsail, main topgallant sail, skysail, and that's that. And now quick through the foremast: foresail, lower fore-topsail, upper fore-topsail . . . (KRUDEWIL *staggers*)

KRUDEWIL:

Everything's rocking, stormy seas, I'm seasick . . . Lower fore-topsail, upper fore-topsail . . . (FRIGATE, *a strapping female in an admiral's uniform with a frigate for a hat, saunters in. She is smoking three cigars by turns and blowing her bosun's whistle*)

FRIGATE:

Lower fore-topsail. Upper fore-topsail. Continue, gentlemen. Continue, you knights of the rail, you steam horses, you coal eaters. Continue!

PEMPELFORT:

Go on, Krudewil, keep your chin up!

KRUDEWIL:

Fore . . . fore . . . t. . . .

PEMPELFORT (*playfully*):

Fore-topsail! It's as easy as pie. Foreroyal, fore-topgallant sail, upper fore-topsail. And now we'll run through the mizzenmast again: mizzen staysail, mizzen-topmast staysail, mizzen-topgallant staysail, mizzen-royal staysail, spanker . . . (KRUDEWIL *sinks into* PEMPELFORT'S *arms*) He's feeling a little sick, sir, it will pass . . .

FRIGATE:

Railsick, seasick! A man with the strength of a whale, who has sailed the seven seas, who was at Trafalgar and the Skaggerak, who's tangled with big fish and little fish—and what does he do? He gets seasick! (*Modestly*) I, a tender Flemish virgin, who was always sitting modestly at her spinning wheel, sniffling because both my hands were busy, I, who used to blush if anyone said "honey child" within ten feet of me, I, in a century when witching and hexing were a popular pastime, was bewitched, turned into a wooden figurehead. Later, after years of piracy, after innumerable naval battles, a leaping dolphin kissed me. That broke the spell, and I turned into an admiral: Lepanto, Trafalgar, Aboukir! I was defeated, sunk, and changed again, this time into the sea serpent that is such a joy to newspaper readers during the summer doldrums . . . Ah, Frigate, how many times more will you have to change your course and go looking for your mutinous crews? (*To* KRUDEWIL *and* PEMPELFORT) You ought to be keel-hauled, tarred and feathered. Let the sharks have what's left. (*She circles around them and whistles*) Anchors aweigh! All hands to starboard! (PEMPELFORT *and* KRUDEWIL *stand facing one another and come to attention. They grab each other by the right ears*) To port! (*By the left ears*) And starboard—port—and starboard—and midships —(*forehead to forehead*) and aft. (*They about-face and stand back to back, head to head*) Midships and now aft again—and aft—and aft!—What's your locomotive called?

PEMPELFORT *and* KRUDEWIL

Frigate!

FRIGATE:
  Course?

PEMPELFORT *and* KRUDEWIL:
  South-southeast.

FRIGATE:
  What do you fire your locomotive with?

PEMPELFORT *and* KRUDEWIL:
  Wind.

FRIGATE:
  Course?

PEMPELFORT *and* KRUDEWIL:
  South-southeast.

FRIGATE:
  What do your swallows look like?

PEMPELFORT *and* KRUDEWIL:
  White, and they live on fish.

FRIGATE:
  What rails do we ride on?

PEMPELFORT:
  The salty kind.

FRIGATE:
  Course?

PEMPELFORT *and* KRUDEWIL:
  South-southeast!

FRIGATE:
  What about Buffalo?

PEMPELFORT *and* KRUDEWIL:
  Where's that?

FRIGATE:
  Where's Buffalo?

PEMPELFORT *and* KRUDEWIL:
  How would we know?

FRIGATE:
  Buffalo?

PEMPELFORT *and* KRUDEWIL:
  Never heard of it.

PEMPELFORT:
  Maybe it's on the North Sea or the Lake of Geneva.

KRUDEWIL:
  It must be some stinking whistle stop.

PEMPELFORT:
  Between Topeka and Keokuk.

KRUDEWIL:
  Without even a school or a drugstore.

PEMPELFORT:
  We wouldn't want to go there. We want to round the
  Cape. We want to jam into the wind on a windjammer.

PEMPELFORT *and* KRUDEWIL:
  Course south-southeast!

FRIGATE (*whistles*):
  Stations! Rig all sails and man the masts! (KRUDEWIL *hoists*
  PEMPELFORT *on his back.* PEMPELFORT *looks out over the
  ocean.* AXEL *comes in from the left, carrying a milk pail.
  He is astonished*)

FRIGATE:
  Calk your hearts, ready harpoons! (*To* AXEL) Stow it,
  cowboy. You take the wind out of my jib. I'm going to
  stop that mouth of yours like a leak. (*She puts two cigars
  in his mouth*) You've got to draw, draw! (AXEL *smokes,*
  FRIGATE *takes a spyglass from her pocket and directs it
  at the locomotive.* PEMPELFORT *has sighted something*) A
  wreck to starboard. No rail, no rudder, all masts lopped
  off. What's become of her jib and mainsail?

PEMPELFORT:
  Whale! Whale! There she blows, there she blows!

FRIGATE:
  That's the seaman's fate. No compass, no port.

PEMPELFORT:
  . . . blows. There she blows.

FRIGATE (*darkly*):

It's my fate too. To drift without anchor, without compass, without a port.

PEMPELFORT:

There, there, there she blows.

FRIGATE (*tears her eyes away from the locomotive. Briskly*):
Where, where, where away?

PEMPELFORT:

There again. There she blows.

FRIGATE:

He's going to sound.

PEMPELFORT:

He's sounding.

FRIGATE:

In stunsails. Down topgallants. Ha, Moby Dick, thine hour and thy harpoon are at hand. Luff a point. The boats!—stand by!

KRUDEWIL:

He's heading straight to leeward.

FRIGATE:

Shut up, man, stand by the braces. Hard down the helm. Brace up! Shiver her!—shiver her. Well done! Boats, boats! (PEMPELFORT *and* KRUDEWIL *mime a rowboat.* FRIGATE *in the stern with spyglass and cigar*) Merrily, merrily, heart's alive, and pull, pull, pull, will ye? pull, can't you? Hurrah for the gold cup of sperm oil . . . There'll be pudding for supper and sauerkraut. Pull, pull, my fine hearts alive . . . crack all your backbones and bite your knives in two . . . Frigate is with you. There, there, there, she blows, pull, she blows, long and strong, she blows (*more softly as she goes out*), long and strong, blows, long and strong, blows, whale, whale, there she blows . . .

AXEL (*slowly shaking his head*):

They're after the cows like horseflies. (*He approaches the locomotive with pail and cigars*) They want to go to Buffalo and all they can do is chase cows. (*He climbs into the cab and whistles for his dog*) Here, Jonah, here. They come out here and chase cows when they want to go to Buffalo. Why shouldn't I take a little trip for a change?— I haven't any friends or relatives in Buffalo, but just for a couple of days, why not? (*He titters and smokes, the engine sends out steam, howls, and starts moving. As it slowly moves off to the right,* AXEL *looks out the window and alternates cigars. The cows moo, the dog barks. A flash and a report in the smokestack. It has got too hot for* KRUDEWIL'S *pistol*)

CURTAIN

The Wicked Cooks

A Drama in Five Acts

Translated by A. Leslie Willson

Cast of Characters

HERBERT SCHYMANSKI, called "The Count"

PETRI, a cook

GRÜN, a cook

VASCO, a cook

STACH, a cook

BENNY, a cook

KLETTERER, a cook

MARTHA, a nurse

THERESE, Vasco's aunt

MRS. KÜHLWASSER, a laundress

Cooks from Kletterer's staff

Act I

(Night: Stage left, a small adjoining room. HERBERT SCHYMANSKI, *called* THE COUNT, *sits writing at a desk before the window. In the center of the stage the cook* PETRI *is hunched on a stool, blowing a gigantic trumpet. The instrument is pointed toward the floor. At every blast from the trumpet the young cook* BENNY *slides partway out of the horn. In the hazy background the silhouette of a bridge)*

BENNY:

Not so loud, Chief! Piano, piano. *(A last trumpet blast and* BENNY, *completely expelled, springs onto his feet and digs his fingers into his ears)* Enough! *(He laughs)* Take a break before you go on.

PETRI:

Don't laugh, young man, it might boomerang. *(*BENNY *keeps on laughing.* PETRI *kicks him)* Don't laugh!

BENNY:

What's the matter now? I can't hear anything any more, Chief. Time to knock off.

PETRI:

Take it away! *(He points at the trumpet)* And bring the hammer. The hammer, and the everyday trumpet.

BENNY:

The hammer?

PETRI:

Exactly. And look! *(He pantomimes a small trumpet)*

BENNY *(whistles meaningfully)*:

Big party, little trumpet! *(He whistles again, takes the stool, rolls the large trumpet off the stage, and returns with a sledge hammer and a little version of the big trumpet.* PETRI *importantly, with arms folded over his chest)*

PETRI:

How's your hearing?

BENNY:

Better already, Chief. I'm all ears!

PETRI:

All right, then we can begin. *(He plays a kind of flourish: in the background a large egg appears. Without rolling, it slides forward)*

BENNY:

Fresh as a daisy. *(He hands* PETRI *the hammer)*

PETRI:

I bet it's still warm. I'm kind of curious, though I ought to know . . . *(He hangs the trumpet around his neck and strikes the egg carefully with the hammer. The egg breaks in the middle and the cook* GRÜN, *a frying pan in each hand, jumps from the shells)* Who else could it have been but Grün?

GRÜN:

What thoughtful chickens! Besides the nourishing yolk, they also furnish the frying pans right off. A little game, Benny? *(He tosses a pan to* BENNY. *They improvise a tennis match.* PETRI *blows the trumpet furiously)*

PETRI:

Stop that stuff! Put those things away! We've got to get going!

GRÜN:

Benny, go get him the shovel. He's in a hurry today. *(*BENNY *stacks the shells and holds them playfully over his head)*

BENNY:

Under whose window shall I lay the eggshells? *(He laughs foolishly.* PETRI *gives him a threatening look.* BENNY *stops laughing, exits quickly, and comes back with a shovel)*

PETRI:

The snotnose! One of these days he's going to laugh his teeth right out of his mouth. (*He blows the trumpet: a cone as tall as a man rises out of the floor*)

GRÜN:

I wonder if there's a mouse in there! (*He nibbles at the cone*) Salt, innocent, common table salt. And so much? Whose soup were you two going to spoil? (*He makes a curtsy*)

> What can be sweeter than salt,
> Recently asked the nanny goat.
> A bell she wore on her throat,
> And started to lick the sole of my shoe,
> To bring my secret into view.
> She cried out and bleated for salt.

(PETRI *takes the shovel from* BENNY)

PETRI:

A really good nanny goat can make even a stone talk.

(*He thrusts the shovel in the salt cone; as though he were jabbed, the cook* VASCO *springs out. The cone collapses*)

VASCO:

No! No! I told ya everything, ya see. More than I even know. (PETRI, GRÜN, *and* BENNY *laugh*)

GRÜN:

Good old Vasco. How nervous he is!

PETRI:

He always has a bad conscience.

BENNY:

Maybe he's in love?

GRÜN:

Who with, anyway?

BENNY:

With Martha.

GRÜN:

And that's why he's in salt up to his ears.

VASCO:

Mr. Petri, those two know me. They know how I feel about her. It's just sympathy, common humanity. (*He chews on his fingernails*)

PETRI:

But, Vasco, do you have to do that? Are you biting your fingernails again? The Count doesn't like it.

GRÜN:

He might get appendicitis. He could die on us. We'd be awfully sad and we'd weep tears, salty, sweet tears.

PETRI (*counts his staff*):

One is still missing!

GRÜN:

What's this? You haven't had enough? You feel you've got to run through that trumpet act again? We know you're musical! It's still ringing in our ears.

PETRI:

But one is missing!

GRÜN:

Fine, but no music!

PETRI:

He's irritable, Grün is, sensitive, nervous, subject to moods. I've got to be considerate, and I'm the Chief. I'm not allowed to blow when I want to. Well, there's another way (*He claps his hands. In the background snow begins to fall heavily on one spot.* PETRI *claps again. The snowfall subsides, stops, and the cook* STACH *emerges from the flakes*)

STACH:

Jesus, in the middle of August. What he can't do, that Petri! (*He makes a snowball, throws it, and hits* BENNY. BENNY *throws back and they carry on like children.* PETRI'S *trumpet call restores order*)

PETRI:

We mustn't forget the purpose of our drill. We are in

danger. Our good reputation seems shaken. People are turning away. They don't like our food any more.

VASCO:

They want to demolish us.

PETRI:

Demolish us and dismantle us, move us out and put us in moth balls.

STACH:

We've become victims! They'll slaughter us. Nowadays they're sticking cooks, not pigs.

PETRI:

We've got to take stock, turn over a new leaf. (*He yells*) And stick together, see? No standing aside. No punishment is too hard for any who . . . (*He looks at the cooks quizzically, one after the other*) Benny, get the canopy! (BENNY *runs out and brings in a black canopy on four poles.* PETRI *and* BENNY *take positions under the canopy. The other cooks form a loose circle*)

PETRI (*singing*):

One cook,

BENNY:

no, two cooks,

PETRI *and* BENNY:

two cooks left the kitchen.

PETRI:

One cook left the house,
walked out into the night,
the night was black, and bashed
his hat in,
an, on, one

BENNY:

two!

PETRI *and* BENNY:

The night is full of cooks!
The night is full of cooks!

(GRÜN *and* VASCO *step under the canopy*)

H

PETRI:

One cook,

BENNY:

two cooks,

GRÜN:

who counts three,

VASCO:

counts four cooks,

ALL FOUR:

and all of them left the kitchen.

GRÜN:

Four cooks from the house away,
like a wicked white bouquet
blooming in the dark of night,
giggling with delight,
delight, delight, delight—

ALL FOUR:

The night is full of cooks!
The night is full of cooks!

(STACH *steps under the canopy*)

STACH:

Five cooks, five bona fide cooks,
they left their kitchen at home.

PETRI *and* BENNY:

And each one has a little spoon,
a small potato is the moon,

GRÜN *and* VASCO:

little dumplings every star,
the sky a sauce as black as tar.

STACH:

As though a man could stir them,
with spoons a man could lure them,
as though they were the soup,
as though the night were soup.

ALL FIVE:

> The night, it is a soup!
> The night, it is a soup!
> (*Slowly they exit*)

PETRI:

> And everywhere the cooks stand,
> the cooks stand, the cooks stand . . .
> (*In the background, many cooks*)

PETRI:

> The night is full of cooks!

ALL:

> The night is full of cooks!

(*In* THE COUNT's *room the light goes up.* THE COUNT *stands up and picks up his letter. While he reads from the letter aloud, cooks appear from time to time in the background with their canopy. Muffled,* PETRI's *trumpet sounds*)

THE COUNT (*at the window*):

How wild they are! That hornblowing! (*He reads*) My dear friend, if you knew what terror you have abandoned me to, you would come and be with me. (*He puts the letter down*) I'm a pretty good liar. Even if he knew, he wouldn't come. He was with us in the beginning, then quick he bought a ticket and got away. And now he writes me these glossy postcards with virtually nothing on them. And I pretend I'm answering. Answering what? His distraught, pencil-scrawled greetings? (*He reads again*) Of course, it was stupid of me. I should never have gone into the kitchen. I should have remained a customer and left the cooking to them. Was it conceit, was it so flattering for me to tie on an apron now and then and show them a thing or two? They begged me. Schuster, the host, wouldn't give up, and he backed up the customers. Now they want the recipe. (*He puts the letter down*) But I won't tell them! How simple it would be just to go and say: Boys, there you have it! Good luck! (*He reads*) And besides, I'm afraid. They frighten me. The way they appear takes my breath away, and it costs me an effort to remain calm. In every snowfall, behind the laundry—anything white, if it's just large enough, conceals a cook. If I see a swan, I distrust it. Even this paper seemed suspicious to me when it was new. I have written very fast! (*He folds the letter, sticks it in an envelope, and addresses it*) How will it go on? They'll give me no peace. They'll hound me. One skirmish will follow the other. Nothing is too petty for them. First they've taken away the glasses from the near-sighted, next they'll expropriate the possessive pronouns. They'll force me to wear a glass tie so they can look into my heart, so they can read what's there—for I will not speak! (*He glances out the window*) It's quieter outside now. Even cooks get tired! (*He throws a scarf around his neck*) Now for a mailbox. I almost believe that all that holds us together nowadays is the mail. (THE COUNT *leaves the room. From the background the cook* VASCO *appears. Both approach the bridge*)

THE COUNT (*hesitates, then gets a grip on himself*):
A riddle! What can that be? It stands on a bridge, is white like a bride, not quite so innocent, and it bites its fingernails?

VASCO (*steps up*):
Count . . .

THE COUNT:
And now it says Count to me. "Count!" I'm not even the clothes rack of a count. Simple, unpretentious, a common man who just tries to get along.

VASCO:
But they all call you that! The customers, Mr. Schuster. Don't he bow and talk soft when the door opens and ya come in? (*He bows*) Ah, the Count, a great honor!

THE COUNT (*laughing*):
But you, my friend, you know my name.

VASCO:

Don't ya say Vasco, too, like that was my name?

THE COUNT:

That's who you are. The great explorer, the man who refuses to believe that the continents are numbered and the seas have been named.

VASCO:

I'm a cook, a cook, a cook all over!

THE COUNT:

Who can deny it?—What do you want?

VASCO:

Well, ya see . . . (*He starts to grab* THE COUNT, *who dodges*)

THE COUNT:

Well?

VASCO:

The recipe, if ya don't mind. Why d'ya keep asking? Don't I always come and say: Hand it over!?

THE COUNT:

And the others?—You shouldn't bite your fingernails. Do you think your great ancestor acted so nervous when he discovered the route to India?

VASCO:

I'm not here to talk about colonies. The recipe! If ya'll be so kind.

THE COUNT:

What will Petri say about that? I mean, does he know that you, in all your splendor and on your own account, lie in wait here for harmless passers-by?

VASCO:

No.

THE COUNT:

I see.

VASCO:

Are ya gonna tell 'im?

THE COUNT:

You're being very foolish.

VASCO:

He won't notice it. He'll think I'm at my aunt's, 'cause she's sick, and Martha . . .

THE COUNT:

What about her?

VASCO:

Please, please, you say it's dangerous to talk too much around here, so tell me quick and I'll be going.

THE COUNT:

Who's with your aunt? Who's taking care of her?

VASCO:

What are ya getting at? Are we gonna talk about sickness here? The soup! The recipe!

THE COUNT:

No, Vasco. It isn't the right night for that. The clouds strike me as purely fortuitous. Go on, run home with your chef's hat or the night will bash it in. Off with you!

(*He claps his hands and takes a few steps.* VASCO *clutches him*)

VASCO:

Why're ya clapping? Am I a chicken that flaps up when somebody claps? Hand it over!

THE COUNT:

My scarf? At once! (*He puts the scarf around* VASCO's *neck*) My tie, my suspenders—but that might be awkward. How about my shoelaces? (VASCO *hands the scarf back wordlessly*) Don't you like it? Do you want—what else do I have? (*He searches himself*)

VASCO (*turned away*):

I won't even use it—except maybe a little for myself. I'll memorize it. I'll say it to myself by heart like a pretty poem in front of the mirror. Also to you, ya see, so that ya can't say: He learned it wrong, Vasco did.

(He laughs and leaps about)

It'll be fun! We can say it to one another and always know what we mean.

(He looks at the silent COUNT)

We can also stand back to back, if you're ashamed or if you're afraid of the way I talk.

THE COUNT:

I'm not afraid of anything. I'm not ashamed of anything. I said no. What more do you want?

VASCO *(vehemently)*:

The paper! What else am I gonna have to do, to make ya hand it over? Want me to climb up the lamppost *(he scrambles up the lamppost)* and grind my teeth? *(He slides down again)* Or go down on my knees *(he kneels)* and beat my chest and say: Pretty please?

THE COUNT:

Are you still talking about the soup?

VASCO *(jumps up)*:

What else would I be talking about? It has a color, I don't know which. Everybody calls it the gray soup, and they come back into the kitchen in their black suits with their blonde ladies and nice smell, and they say to me: "Cook it for us, Vasco!" Well, what am I supposed to do? Am I gonna admit I can't? I'm a bad cook? Ask the Count, if you please. He knows how to make it. He made it two, three times, and the customers went wild.

THE COUNT:

Mr. Schuster asked me to.

VASCO:

And now they're asking me to. *(He bends down and scratches at the ground)* Here, am I gonna take dirt and stir it in, so that it has color, the gray soup?

THE COUNT:

I didn't call it that.

VASCO:

But people do.

THE COUNT:

You shouldn't listen. It doesn't have a name at all. (*He
walks back and forth, with* VASCO *following him*) All right.
I admit, all kinds of names occur to me. November soup,
Phoenix soup, Gray Eminence. Yes, imagine! I almost
named it after old Holstein—he was a great cook!

VASCO (*vehemently*):

It don't matter what it's called! Do I cook with sound?
Do I taste with my ear?

(MARTHA, *in the uniform of a nurse, joins them from
the left*)

MARTHA:

Stephan!

(*Both give a start*)

VASCO (*angrily*):

What's the matter? Why're ya running around at night?
Why ain't ya at the hospital where they need ya?

MARTHA:

The head nurse let me go so that I can take care of your
aunt.

VASCO:

Well, why ain't ya there, giving her her medicine?

MARTHA:

I *was* with your aunt. She asked about you. After all, you
wanted to . . .

VASCO:

Aunt, aunt, always aunt. How many times do I have to
hear it? Say aunt a hundred times, real fast, and then ask
yourself, what is that? Something to lay down, set up,
throw away!

MARTHA:

Stephan!

VASCO (*covers his ears*):

I can't listen when she complains like that.—Didn't I tell
ya not to? Is my name a hook that anybody can hang
his gripes on? Don't ya see who's standing there?

MARTHA:

Please excuse us.

THE COUNT:

Don't mention it, child. What we're saying here are words falling into the water. Not even a fish would be interested.

MARTHA:

Shall I go now?

THE COUNT:

Vasco will go with you. He's so on the job, the good fellow, he forgot his aunt.

VASCO:

Forgot nothing! She's got to leave now, not bother us!

MARTHA:

But, but . . .

VASCO:

Are ya gonna say that word again, like I had an ear for it? Don't ya know what he's gonna tell me? D'ya want to make me mad? (*He raises his hand to hit her, but* THE COUNT *restrains him*)

THE COUNT:

Please go now! (*She backs out reluctantly*)

VASCO:

Stephan'll teach her to come here in the flesh and open her mouth.

THE COUNT:

You're more severe than you intend to be. (*He lets him go*) Calm down!

VASCO:

Why does she come when I'm here?

THE COUNT:

She was talking about your aunt.

VASCO:

Phooey! She thinks that means something to me, thinks I'll drop everything and crawl into her net.

THE COUNT:

You're not fair. After all, she is your aunt and . . .

VASCO:

My aunt, your aunt! Am I supposed to own her? Ya want me to run around saying: I have an aunt? Isn't the nurse enough? Did ya see her face? When I look at her I get all mixed up. I forget important things. She affects me like an anaesthetic.

THE COUNT:

You're right, you do look rather tired.

VASCO:

Okay, okay. (*He stares absently into the distance*)

THE COUNT:

Well, then, I suppose I'll . . . and you ought to also. Right, Vasco? We've chatted enough.

VASCO:

What about?

THE COUNT:

Nothing important.—I'm going, I still have to take this letter to the mailbox. (*He starts to leave.* VASCO *looks up*)

VASCO:

Letter? (*He holds him forcibly*) What's written in it? Is it . . . is it . . . ? (*He presses him against the bridge railing*)

THE COUNT:

No, absolutely not. You mean . . .

VASCO:

Now I know! (*He laughs*) Now is the time. Now you'll tell. This is the only ear around. (*He shakes him*) Tell me—well? Well?

THE COUNT (*laughing*):

Do I have to chat some more? Well, what do you want to hear? That you're a great cook? That there's nothing you don't cook to a T? That you stir me?—But what spoon doesn't stir me?—Well, never mind! (*He tries to free himself, but* VASCO *clutches him tighter and shoves him half over the bridge railing*) Come, come! A boxing match without a crowd? I'm not Jacob, and you would be a measly angel. (*Tries to shove him away.* VASCO'S *hat falls from the bridge*) Vasco! Vasco! I must tell you something in confidence.

VASCO (*stops*):

Well?

THE COUNT:

You've lost your hat. Where will it float to?

VASCO (*lets him go and leans over the railing*):

It don't look right in the water.

THE COUNT (*straightens out his clothing*):

Poor fellow, what an effort! But why? Were you going to drown me and the recipe? Were you about to cook for the fish? (*He too leans over the railing*) It really doesn't look right. Do you think I would have looked better down there? Of course, maybe life under water is very nice. Under the water it doesn't rain, under the water it's calm and bullet-proof. Nobody calling out the headlines. In short, you live more simply under water. (*He claps* VASCO *on the shoulder*)

VASCO:

You're pulling my leg!

THE COUNT:

How could I? There are things in this world that I don't find at all amusing. For example, that you wanted to buy me. That you tried to play fast and loose with my private little bit of life. Watch, now, and tell me how much you think this breathing in and out is worth. (*He jumps up onto the bridge railing, moves very adroitly on it, and even does a few tricks*)

VASCO:

Stop that stuff on the railing!

THE COUNT:

Don't you like it? Something else? Oh, yes! The letter!

(*He pulls the letter out of his pocket*) You wanted to know . . . I'll send it after your hat, so they can chat, the two of them. (*He throws the letter from the bridge*)

VASCO:

Come on down now!

THE COUNT:

I should patent that invention. I could get rich with it. Letter boxes with flushing action.

VASCO:

I'm pleading with ya!

THE COUNT:

Oh, give me another minute! I feel so independent up here, so inventive and free in spirit. You could amalgamate the post office and the waterworks, reduce the whole administrative apparatus considerably . . .

VASCO (*pulls him down from the railing*):

I can't watch.

THE COUNT:

How sensitive you can be!

VASCO:

Count, sir . . .

THE COUNT:

No, no longer Count. Or say what you please, call the soup what you please . . . All right, so you won't cry.—It's a cabbage soup, just an ordinary cabbage soup. Except I put a very precise amount of very special ashes into it. Although there's nothing special needed to get special ashes. Now, go, Vasco! With or without a hat, you don't look right here. (*He crosses the bridge toward the right, turns once more*) A cook on a bridge at night, that doesn't look right. Even two, three or four, five cooks. Believe me, even five of the best of all cooks, with that whetted moon in the bargain . . . (*He shakes his head*) Also you shouldn't bite your nails! (THE COUNT *exits swiftly. The cook* STACH *runs onstage from the left*)

STACH:

Jesus, you're a sight! Nothing on your head, and you're biting again. Didn't you hear what he said? (VASCO *turns away from him*) What are you looking at? Is there anything to look at? He's gone!

VASCO:

He's going like not one soul was standing here.

STACH:

Two!

VASCO:

His back don't care about me.

STACH:

Care about us! Two are standing here! And I tell you, it's a good thing I'm standing here and not Petri. (*He nudges him*) You must look here, not there, where there's nothing.

VASCO (*turns slowly*):

Whether one is standing here, or two, he'll finish us all. He comes with his flat feet and he's the smart one. Says Vasco to me and to you says Stach. Petri, he says, and Grün. Slaps us on the shoulder a little. With one hand or the other he slaps us, it don't matter. He'll finish us, finish us.

STACH:

Well, let's finish him.

VASCO:

But even if we finish him ten times, and real slow, he'll put an end to us! (*He leans over the bridge railing*)

STACH:

Don't do that! It's not good for your eyes.

VASCO:

Maybe it caught on something.

STACH (*laughing*):

Or somebody was standing down there, fishing with a pole.

(VASCO *straightens up and* STACH *retreats*) Did I say I was fishing?

VASCO:

You'll give it to me, if you've got something.

STACH:

I haven't got a thing. (*He goes through his clothing*) There, there—well, have I got it? Why are we talking about the hat, let's talk about the Count, or better yet, about Martha. She's a nurse, you're a cook. Monotonous! Too much white! What could you two talk about when you're together? Would you say: "Martha, what's that, flu or nosebleed?" Would she say: "Vasco"—no, "Stephan," she'd say . . .

VASCO:

You shut up right now!

STACH:

You, if you hit me, I'll tell Petri!

VASCO:

Get outta here!

STACH:

But I can't leave you here alone like this—with a bare head.

VASCO (*grabs him and shakes him*):

Am I gonna get you! (*He picks up a rock and starts to throw it.* STACH *runs away, but stops momentarily*)

STACH:

Now watch out, I tell you, watch out! (STACH *exits.* VASCO *throws the rock from the bridge*)

VASCO:

Plop, like that's a word. (*He starts to exit right.* MARTHA *approaches him with a package under her arm. They confront one another silently for a moment*) Did you two talk? Answer me, ya must have met him! Did he say that he's mad? Don't stand there like something left over!

MARTHA:

I was at Mrs. Kühlwasser's.

VASCO:

But ya must have met him, if ya just came from . . . What's the matter with Mrs. Kühlwasser?

MARTHA:

The laundry. (*She indicates the package*)

VASCO:

Ready?

MARTHA:

Not everything, just . . . (*He takes the package from her and opens it quickly*)

VASCO:

Why didn't ya tell me right away what ya got? (*He puts a chef's hat on his head*) Is it all right like this?

MARTHA:

What have you done with the other one? Stephan, what have you done to the . . .

VASCO:

I didn't do nothing. He's alive and still won't say a word. —What's wrong with my aunt?

MARTHA:

She's asking for you.

VASCO:

I don't know whether it'll be good for me to see her die. Maybe I'll have to take my hat off again and not be a cook for five minutes. (*With* MARTHA *ahead, they both exit left*)

CURTAIN

Act II

(*The apartment of* VASCO'S AUNT: *In the room on the left
the* AUNT *is sitting half up in bed. Over the bed hangs a
cuckoo clock. A crucifix in the left corner of the room.
Right of the bed, a small mirror. In the empty room on
the right hang drying bed sheets. In front, to the far right,
stands a large white-tile stove with a seat. In the middle
of the room stands a chair. The room on the left is lighted
brighter than the one on the right.* MARTHA *and* VASCO
enter from the left. The cuckoo clock calls irregularly)

VASCO:

Is that thing still cuckooing? Why don't somebody take
it down and throw it out?

MARTHA:

She says it calls out the right time.

AUNT:

Is that you, my child?

MARTHA:

I've brought Stephan along for you, do you hear, Auntie?

AUNT:

Oh? Was he in church, too?

MARTHA (*to* VASCO):

Please!

AUNT:

Look at him, child, and tell me whether he was.

VASCO:

I've caught cold.

AUNT:

So you were there, after all. Well, how was it?

VASCO:

Like always, drafty, cold.

AUNT:

Martha dear, why doesn't he tell me how it was?

VASCO:

But I did! Just a few people, and they hacked like they'd gone to church just to cough all they wanted to.

AUNT:

And you, did you pray?

VASCO:

As long as I was there.

AUNT:

To whom?

VASCO:

First to St. Anthony, 'cause I lost something, and then, like always, to the Blessed Virgin.

AUNT:

What did you lose, Stephan?

VASCO:

Oh, these questions! Small stuff, nothing important!

AUNT:

But first you . . .

VASCO:

To St. Anthony. Why not? But then I went to her.

AUNT:

And?

VASCO:

No and! Do ya think she chatted with me?

AUNT:

Stephan, Stephan! What's that supposed to mean? There was a time when you always used to come and tell me things.

VASCO (*laughing*):

Yeah, there was. I had different ears then. Then I heard

'em sing, the angels sing. And the Blessed Virgin told me what a virgin is.

AUNT:

Such a nice child you were. So reverent, so pious. (*The cuckoo clock calls*) Did you hear how it called, Martha dear? Fifteen times!

VASCO:

Seventeen, Auntie, ya left two out. (*The* AUNT *sits up*)

AUNT:

Ahhhh! There Stephan goes again! Always the know-it-all. He comes in and says I'm wrong. Go away, get out! He always lies, and he won't tell me what he lost. He never was with the Blessed Virgin, maybe with St. Anthony, but not with Our Blessed Virgin. (*She sinks back*)

VASCO:

I just don't know what you're after! Ya counted wrong. Anyway, why not? After all, you're sick in bed.

MARTHA:

The next time we'll count together, all right? Or I'll take it along tomorrow and have it repaired. Maybe there's not very much wrong, and you can get it back again real soon.

VASCO:

D'ya hear, Auntie? I'll pay for it. Or d'ya want a new one? Tell us! (*To* MARTHA) She can't hear a thing, or don't want to. What a stupid! Like I can't count. That still mixes her up. There's no cuckoo in there, that's a dog. It don't cuckoo, it barks.

AUNT (*in a firm voice*):

Take your hat off, Stephan! You take your hat off this instant! (VASCO *takes his hat off*) Sit down on the bed! Not there, at the foot end. You look wicked without a hat! (VASCO *jumps up*)

VASCO:

Well, I can put it back on!

AUNT:

On the bed, I said. (*He sits down*) No, no, no, there's no sense in that. You look wicked with the hat on, too. I'd hoped that without it you'd look less wicked.

MARTHA:

You're getting excited. Shall we wait next door? It'd be better.

AUNT:

Phooey! Why do you look like that?—Stephan! Come closer! Are you still with Petri? Are you still a cook? Do you still go over there when the cooks meet?

VASCO:

Well, why not?

AUNT:

My brother—you know, your father. You must never forget that my brother Karl was your father.

VASCO:

Oh yeah, sure! Now she's gonna start that story again!

AUNT:

Your father was a cook too. Lordy, what a cook he was! Ordered me all over the place, he did—always stood around slapping me. Just think, Martha dear, he slapped me! Why are cooks so wicked? Does the spoon make them wicked? When they stir, does that make them wicked?

MARTHA:

Listen, Auntie! He's come here to visit you, and he was looking forward to it.

AUNT (*giggles*):

Looking forward, was he? Oho! He comes here and he's jolly and he won't tell me what he prayed and why cooks are like that and what he lost that he should go to St. Anthony and not to the Blessed Virgin.

VASCO:

But I told you . . .

AUNT:

Quiet! Just what is it about them? When they have their
hats on, they're wicked. If they take them off, they're
still wicked. Holy Mary and Joseph, what's it all mean?
And I always thought, when a cook takes his hat off,
he's a Christian. Do you hear, Stephan, a Christian! (*She
weeps whimperingly and* VASCO *jumps up*)

VASCO:

Is that all? Why do I come here? All the time catechism,
just all the time catechism and embarrassment.

MARTHA:

Please, Stephan!

VASCO:

Stephan, please, please! Stephan! And what about her?
She don't have a name. She's my aunt, and that's that.
Did Papa call her aunt? Therese he called her! And when
he yelled Therese, she knew what was coming. And you,
why do you say Auntie, too? Are you her relative, is she
your aunt? No! Fine, you're living at the hospital. They
all call each other sister, brother, or aunt as far as I care.
But is this a hospital? No! Well, why ain't you and her,
too, why ain't ya both . . .

MARTHA:

She wants to . . . *here*, Stephan. Please try to understand
that.

VASCO:

But you. You're off duty? For how long?

MARTHA:

The nurses just said I ought to take care of her, it was
the right thing to do. She was so nice, the head nurse.

VASCO:

Oh, she was nice, was she? And you are, too, huh? And
what about me, what am I?

MARTHA:

I didn't mean it that way.

VASCO:

I'm a wicked man. Well, didn't she say that?

MARTHA:

Be quiet now! She's getting upset. The fever's coming on.

VASCO (*puts on his hat and takes a stance before the small mirror*):

D'ya see? There! Hat on, wicked cook! Hat off, wicked cook! And from behind, too, and from the side, from the left, from above—I ask ya!—and from way off, always wicked! What kind of a word is that? Is that a word like hat's a word, or stovepipe? Wicked, is that a soup? Is it a white fish crying out for lemon? Is it a pork kidney, when it gets a sudden shock in the skillet? Is it salt? Is salt wicked? Ain't salt Christian? And the chicken, when it's stuffed with truffles and a bit of sage? (*He stares into the mirror*)

AUNT:

Stephan! You have your hat on again.

VASCO:

It don't matter, ya said.

AUNT:

Does he have it on, child?

MARTHA:

No, Auntie, he's taken it off.

VASCO:

On, I have it on!

AUNT:

Come here! (VASCO *takes a stance before the bed*)

VASCO:

What's on your mind?

AUNT:

The hat!

VASCO (*throws the hat down.* MARTHA *picks it up*):

It's a laugh when you order me around like that!

AUNT:

Kneel down!

VASCO:

Jeezmary, what next?

AUNT:

Knock him in the knees, Martha dear! Knock him, if he won't do it.

MARTHA (*softly*):

Well, do it!

VASCO (*kneels indolently*):

Is this good enough?

AUNT:

Begin!

VASCO:

You don't want me to pray *here?*

AUNT:

Don't look at me, look over there, where the Lord is. Well, make it snappy!

VASCO:

I can't think of anything to say.

AUNT:

Pray the Sorrowful. In the name of the Father—well, go on, go on! (*The cuckoo clock calls for a long time irregularly.* VASCO *jumps up*)

VASCO:

There, let the cuckoo pray! He learned it, knows it by heart. He'll pray more than enough for you. The Sorrowful and the Joyful, rosaries and coffee rings, and I don't know what all. (*He runs without his hat into the room on the right and sits down on the chair*)

MARTHA:

Stephan!

AUNT (*laughing*):

There he goes, running off with his feelings hurt.

MARTHA:

What's the matter with him?

AUNT:

You should ask! Do you want to be like him, always asking questions? It has made him melancholy, and that's the work of Satan.

MARTHA:

You're just saying that, Auntie. I don't know.

AUNT:

Oh yes! That's the way they are, those cooks. Always a bit melancholy. (*She laughs*)

MARTHA:

Are you feeling better now? You're laughing again.

AUNT:

I'd just like to know why he always bites his fingernails!

(*In the first room the light dims; in the second it comes up.* VASCO *straightens up. While he speaks, the objects about him—the bed sheets and the tile stove—become hazy*)

VASCO:

Why is she dying like that? She don't even try! Is she pulling my leg now, and the others, too? They call me Stephan and Vasco. *He* was the first one to come and say: "Your name is Stephan? That's stupid! Vasco, Vasco, explorer, traveler to India, spice fetishist!"—Haven't I been learning alla time? And Papa, didn't he say one Sunday while Mamma was asleep: "Go to Mr. Petri!" And on Monday I goes, and he gives me money to take along for the white uniform, and I'm all choked up when I says to Petri: "That's for the white uniform. I'm supposed to learn your trade. And Papa says hello!" Boy, did Petri laugh when I came in, and then he stood there all those years and roared do this and do that, and that's the way to do it—and now my aunt lies there screaming: "Take off your hat!" (*He clutches his head and springs up*) Where is it? If Petri saw how bare I am on top, if he saw that! (*The cook* PETRI *appears from behind a bed sheet, a small trumpet under his arm.* VASCO *sinks back in his chair and raises his hands in fright.* PETRI *blows a few soft notes*)

PETRI:

What do I see? Somebody's sitting there, and he's scared. Why? How come? Maybe because he has nothing on his head? Did my few sweet notes sweep him bare on top? Vasco, where is your hat?

VASCO:

My aunt, Mr. Petri.

PETRI:

Your aunt, always your aunt!

VASCO:

I was standing beside her. It was hot 'cause the windows were shut . . .

PETRI:

And then you threw it away.

VASCO:

No!

PETRI:

Tell the truth! You took it off and flung it away, away, someplace out there in a field of turnips or from a bridge —away, into the night, as though the night were a drawer for chef's hats. (*He blows a note*) What will the one who finds it think?

VASCO:

Nobody'll find it. (PETRI *polishes the trumpet*)

PETRI:

He'll pick it up and say: "What a ridiculous thing! Alone and solitary as a twin whose brother has died, some cook is running through the night, armed with his little spoon, and wants to make himself a dark soup."

VASCO:

Of course not, where would I get that idea?

PETRI (*Trumpet sound*):

    A so-called ash-gray soup!

VASCO:

    It must be a mix-up, a mistake.

PETRI:

    That's exactly what the lucky hat-finder will say: "A really regrettable mistake! How can one wretched cook hope to make soup out of this cloudy night? Yes, if there were several, maybe five, then perhaps. But as it is?"

VASCO:

    If ya don't mind, Mr. Petri . . .

PETRI:

    Did he perhaps intend to stir the night till it was done? Or did he intend to let it boil over?

VASCO:

    God strike me dead if I ever even thought of it!

PETRI:

    It would also be extremely dangerous. (VASCO *falls on his knees*)

VASCO:

    Oh, do believe me! I was with my aunt and, and . . .

PETRI:

    What's this? A little prayer? Do you think I'm the Blessed Virgin or St. Anthony that people pray to if they lose their hats, for instance?

VASCO:

    Oh, please, Mr. Petri!

PETRI:

    Stand up! (*Vasco gets up*) Oh, please! Oh, a nice round O. Have you also become a poet, a man who says "O"? Always O, when he can think of nothing else? Quiet! (*Trumpet sound*) I'm on to you! You wanted to invent, to imagine—but we can, too! Grün! Grün! (*The cook* GRÜN *leaps down from the tile stove as though he had always been up there*)

GRÜN:

That wasn't so easy, you know!

PETRI:

What? Didn't you get everything?

GRÜN:

Yes, yes, yes! Only it wasn't easy.

PETRI:

But you have enough?

GRÜN:

All weighed out. Nine bags.

PETRI (*laughing*):

Boys, boys! (*Trumpet sound*) Come on out! Stach, come on out! (*The cook* STACH *rolls out from under the stove bench*)

STACH:

The spoon! (*He brandishes a spoon*)

GRÜN:

That's the ticket! Get Benny out here now. If possible, without music. (PETRI *lowers the trumpet*)

PETRI:

Ta-ta-ta, for Mr. Grün! (*He claps his hands*) Let's go! Come here with the fire, boy! Get going! (*The large stove door springs open. The young cook* BENNY *climbs deftly out of the stove, provided with a pot and a flame*)

BENNY:

Well, sir, how do I do it?

PETRI:

It'll boil right away. It's just fine. (*Trumpet sound*) My dear Grün, what have you dreamed up? (*With his spoon* GRÜN *begins to shovel from his bags into the pot*)

GRÜN:

Dreamed up is good. Am I a poet that I dream up things? I did it by computation. I added, I subtracted, and divided it by something you can't say out loud. (*All except* VASCO *laugh*)

VASCO:

If ya don't mind, what's cooking?

GRÜN:

Look at old Vasco, and without a hat!

STACH:

He makes up for it by biting his nails, as if they were an appetizer.

PETRI:

Do you think, too, that he looks awful without a head covering?

GRÜN:

I'd almost say he looks naked.

BENNY:

He'll catch cold.

STACH:

Well, where did he leave his hat?

BENNY:

Maybe he sold it or made his little fiancée a bib with it.

STACH:

Why does she need a bib, if she's a nurse? (*All except* vasco *laugh*)

PETRI:

Joking aside, let's not be mean to him.

GRÜN:

We ought to be big-hearted and let him in on what is bubbling so cheerfully and slowly gaining color here in the pot.

STACH:

Tell him, tell Vasco! He's always a little bit curious.

PETRI:

Where shall we begin? Maybe there, in the blue packet.

GRÜN:

Something spicy. But it doesn't add spice, instead it makes it dull.

PETRI:

And that?

GRÜN:

That makes you sad.

BENNY:

And this?

GRÜN:

That draws bees and is good for diabetes.

STACH:

Jesus, I don't like any of it. What about that?

GRÜN:

That? That's the most expensive of all the varieties of rice. Pin seeds. Boys, when that flowers, then there's a real springtime! All the tailors and seamstresses, housewives, and old maids, all who have anything to do with pins—they'll all come out and oh and ah about the splendor of the blossoms and pick themselves a bouquet. (*They laugh*)

VASCO (*uneasily*):

Who's that *for,* if ya don't mind?

STACH:

O Lord, the little innocent! (*Trumpet sound*)

BENNY (*imitating* VASCO's *tone of voice*):

Who's that *for,* if ya don't mind?

STACH:

Well, if he doesn't suspect what's going on. He's a dreamer, a dreamer.

VASCO (*he jumps up, but drops again into the chair*):

I'm wide awake. I'm a cook, not a dreamer.

GRÜN:

The opposite of a cook is a chimney sweep. Shall we make one out of him?

PETRI:

We can find a chimney quick enough.

GRÜN:

A rope, too.

STACH:

Let's let him rise up like smoke for sausages.

BENNY:

What'll Martha say about that?

VASCO:

You all leave now, this is my aunt's place.

GRÜN (*whistles derisively*):

He's gonna throw us out!

PETRI:

And the way he says that: my aunt's.

STACH:

Are you the owner of your aunt? Is that a way for a bright
boy to talk? You'd do better to tell us where your hat is.

VASCO (*points to the first room*):

It's in there, in there.

STACH:

In where?

VASCO:

Well, in my aunt's room!

PETRI:

The old lady again. (STACH *and* BENNY *dance and sing*)

STACH *and* BENNY:

> Where, oh where does my hat repose?
> With my sickly auntie.
> With my hat, oh she rubbed her nose,
> Nose of my sickly auntie.
> Auntinose and sicklynose,
> Hat repose, rubbed her nose.
> If the cook a hat he had,
> As a cook he wouldn't be bad.
> Where, oh where does my hat repose?
> With my sickly auntie . . . (*Trumpet sound*)

PETRI:

Enough of that! Do you want to upset the pot?

STACH:

Holy Joseph, that's all we need!

PETRI:

Ready, Grün? Our pal is hungry. (VASCO *winces*)

GRÜN:

Ready!

PETRI (*to* STACH):

Get set . . .

STACH:

Me?

PETRI:

Well, make it snappy!

STACH:

Jesus, can't Benny?

PETRI:

Follow the script! So, let's go! (*Solemn pose*) Spoon?

STACH:

Is no pantaloon!

PETRI:

Stir spoon about?

STACH:

Empty it out!

PETRI:

Spoon all ashine?

STACH:

Thank Grace divine, for food and wine! (*All but* VASCO *laugh*)

PETRI:

That's fine. So, little friend. Remember what I taught you?—Not a word!—Don't you remember that a cook . . . now, go on . . .

VASCO:

Never ever alone at night . . .

PETRI:

Where is your hat? Fifteen seconds. (*He pulls out his watch*)

VASCO:

I, I . . .

GRÜN:

Get it out, my boy!

PETRI:

Just bite your nails, that's supposed to help.

STACH:

Tell us where it is!

BENNY:

Or you get a spoonful! Five seconds left.

VASCO:

My aunt, please, my aunt . . .

STACH:

Jesus, now he's going to have to swallow it.

VASCO (*screams*):

No! No! Martha! (*The cooks retreat quickly and soundlessly and disappear behind the bed sheets. The stove closes.* VASCO *jumps up as* MARTHA *enters the room*)

MARTHA:

Did you call me, Stephan?

VASCO:

I was dreaming. The bed sheets were moving, the stove was alive and came toward me.

MARTHA:

Now, you see, it's nothing.

VASCO:

Yes. (*He gropes over the sheets*) Where's my hat?

MARTHA:

You forgot it in there. (*She hands him his hat*)

VASCO (*puts the hat on*):

How is she?

MARTHA:

She's resting.

VASCO:

Does she still count, when the clock cuckoos?

MARTHA:

Come now, it's late.

VASCO:

To your place? Will it be quiet at your place? Ya won't ask me questions? And ya won't listen to me? You'll think: Well, that's something else talking there? And ya won't talk when it's all quiet everywhere, and you'll hold your breath? (*The cuckoo clock calls for a long time*) What's wrong with that thing?

MARTHA:

You mustn't count, please.

VASCO:

It's so hard not to count along, and simply to believe how late it is.

CURTAIN

Act III

(The kitchen: Behind a dirty, white wall, in rising cooking steam, are seen the heads of the cooks. On the front side of the wall hang several used hand towels. In the foreground the cook PETRI *sits on a stool, wrapping up his trumpet)*

PETRI:

It's just a mystery to me. How could that possibly happen? Benny! Benny! I must have dropped it or knocked it against . . .

BENNY *(steps in front of the wall and desultorily dries his hands)*:

Does it have a sore throat? Must it go to the doctor?

PETRI:

Something like that. Take it to Moser! And see that you get back here quickly. Have 'em pound out the dents and that's that. And don't forget to say who sent you. Tell him hello and ask if it won't be ready by this evening—I'll be needing it. Say we're having a party.

BENNY:

And you're going to play a solo. *(He takes the trumpet)*

PETRI:

Run, now! (BENNY *goes, turns around)*

BENNY:

What I was gonna ask. What's wrong today, anyway? Trouble?

PETRI:

Will you just . . . ! (BENNY *exits.* GRÜN *steps in front of the wall, dries his hands, and takes out a notebook)*

GRÜN:

> You didn't let your pea-shooter get out of reach, by any chance?

PETRI:

> If by pea-shooter you mean my trumpet, then you saw right. What's up?

GRÜN:

> We have to get the menu ready. I'm supposed to strike out the fricassee.

PETRI:

> Does he have any other wishes?

GRÜN:

> Not enough soups.

PETRI (*incensed*):

> Well, is this a soup kitchen? Put red beets on the stove. We'll make the Polish soup. Thirty cents. How about bouillabaisse?

GRÜN:

> But not on Tuesday!

PETRI:

> Put down borscht, thirty cents. With sour cream, thirty-five.—Of course, I thought something was cooking yesterday. He was in such a hurry, that young gentleman. Without even changing, all of a sudden he was gone.

GRÜN:

> Did you send Stach after him?

PETRI:

> Naturally! We can't let him get away with that. If Schuster finds out we're breaking up, so to speak . . . —Put down something for fricassee, and eighty-five cents.

GRÜN:

> Curried chicken or calf's liver?

PETRI:

> Put down chicken.—Anyway, Stach doesn't think he had any luck. They argued.

GRÜN:

That whole thing is stupid. Schuster overestimates the situation. Five weeks from now and the customers won't even remember the soup any longer.

PETRI:

It's wrong to assume that he'd be concerned about the customers. Be honest, Grün. Why are we knocking ourselves out?—Oh, well!

GRÜN:

Another soup! (*Exiting*)

PETRI:

Soupe d'oignons. Grate some Parmesan. Thirty-five cents. (*Exits behind the wall*)

(*A trapdoor rises. The cook* STACH *comes out of the cellar. He carries a bowl on his shoulder. In the bowl lies a whole pig's head*)

STACH:

It's nice in the cellar. Now I'll make some jellied meat. What do I care what they gripe about. (*He puts the bowl down*) You have it good. They don't hound you any longer. I—I had to follow him and tell later what happened. And now all hell's broken loose. I'll put my tail between my legs and say I don't know a thing. Here— I'll be like this pig's head, lie in the jelly all cut up real little. Then let 'em guess what's in the jellied meat. (*He laughs and starts to take the bowl again.* VASCO *steps in front of the wall and dries his hands. They confront one another silently*)

STACH:

Well, you?

VASCO:

Do they know anything? (*He seizes him*) I asked if they know anything!

STACH:

Not a thing!

VASCO:

Listen . . . !

STACH:

How can I listen when you're tugging at me?

VASCO:

You went to see them, chatted a little. (*Lets him go*)

STACH:

I did nothing.

VASCO (*shoves him*):

You're a perfect innocent. Did nothing, are nothing! And Petri? Why's he looking around with moisture in his eyes?

STACH:

Maybe some secret sorrow.

VASCO:

You shut up, or . . .

STACH:

Jesus, right away you start threatening me! What'll I tell him? Aren't we two together? Didn't we stand like brothers on the bridge? And he went away, and we both thought: What a couldn't-care-less back he has!

VASCO:

Schuster talked to Petri, and after that to Grün.

STACH:

Those three are really worried.

VASCO:

We should be worried! Ya gotta understand, we can't all go. Five's too many! He'll only laugh if he sees five of us.

STACH:

And two, won't he laugh then?

VASCO:

He always laughs a little. But two are not so bad. He don't think much of a crowd of people.

STACH:

Well, and if he sees a crowd? Not just five, but . . .

VASCO (*grabs him*):

You mean Kletterer. Man, if ya go to him . . .

STACH:

Watch out—Petri! (*Both dry their hands awkwardly.*
PETRI *joins them and likewise dries his hands*)

PETRI:

So busy? What can be so important, to make you so diligent?

STACH:

Maybe a jellied meat—the pig is entirely in agreement.

PETRI (*laughs*):

There the two of you stand, letting one another in on
the secrets of preparing jellied meat.

VASCO:

Of course not! We were talking about Martha.

PETRI:

That's even better. Grün, come here quick! (GRÜN *in front
of the wall*)

GRÜN:

Aren't there enough of you standing there already? (*He
dries his hands*)

PETRI:

Far too few! Listen closely, the story's worth it. These two
otherwise diligent cooks are standing here talking about
jellied meat and Martha, also about Martha and jellied
meat, maybe even nicely one after the other: pig's head,
Martha, jellied meat, and fried potatoes, and afterwards
Martha again because she's so pretty, and for dessert an
oatmeal gruel without salt. (STACH *slinks away*)

GRÜN:

I call that worth listening to. Well, how is she?

VASCO:

All right, please! You're joking 'cause we're having a little chat here.—But where's . . . ?

PETRI:

Gone—he's having a little chat with his pig's head. But
enough of this foolishness! Seriously, how is Martha,

anyway? Does she sleep well, enjoy her food, shoes too
tight? Huh? And at the hospital? Does she have to take
pulses, empty bedpans, give enemas? Well. what does
she do there all day? Does she simply run around and
show her pretty face? Or weren't you two talking about
her at all?

GRÜN:

You say Martha, but what were you really talking about?

VASCO:

You can believe me, Mr. Petri. We were talking . . .

PETRI:

Well?

VASCO:

. . . about my aunt's illness.

PETRI:

How everything fits together! Jellied meat, Martha,
Auntie.

GRÜN:

And what's the name of your uncle?

PETRI:

Not so fast! First, Vasco, your aunt.

VASCO:

You must know, she's real sick. I sat up with her all last
night. She don't talk any longer.

GRÜN:

What a shame! But maybe Martha does?—Why are you
so scared?

VASCO:

What have I got to do with her?

GRÜN:

If you can figure that out, go ahead! I mention the name
of his sweet fiancée and right away the even sweeter
husband-to-be gets scared.

PETRI:

Maybe because his aunt's still as a mouse, while Martha

now and then has a bit to say. (VASCO *is restless*) Don't
you think, if we're real nice to her . . . (VASCO *starts to
leave*) . . . she would come to see us? Stay here! (*He
holds* VASCO)

GRÜN:

We'd have a real little chat.—What's the matter with
him, anyway?

VASCO:

The laundry's back, ya know.

GRÜN:

We're talking about coffee and cakes—he thinks he has
to talk about the laundry.—Now just stay here! We'll perk
her some coffee, though coffee is not one of our special-
ties. A piece of apple cake . . .

PETRI:

With whipped cream, generous as we are.

GRÜN:

That'd go well with her pretty, modest nurse's cap. We'd
get along cozily and still stay decent. We'd just happen
to start talking.

VASCO:

She don't know nothing.

GRÜN:

What doesn't she know anything about?

VASCO:

What I'm saying is, she won't get it into her head that
my aunt has to go to the hospital, and that . . .

PETRI:

Enough about your aunt! What doesn't she know anything about?

VASCO:

About anything!

PETRI:

Come, come, who'd be so tactless as to call his little
fiancée a nitwit. He'll never be a gentleman. We—

we must rise to the occasion and, as for the honor of his fiancée, must—how do you put it?

GRÜN:

Rescue it or restore it. We must do something for the lady.

PETRI:

And at once, too. Is Benny back yet? Benny, Benny! (BENNY *steps in front of the wall, a frying pan in each hand*) Well, can it be bent back into shape?

BENNY:

Not worth mentioning, Moser said—barely an hour.

PETRI:

Then run, get Martha, and on your way back, take care of that. But be nice to her! (*He takes the frying pans from him and gives one to* GRÜN)

BENNY:

I'll do my best. What are you doing?

GRÜN:

Very stylish tennis, till the young lady comes.

BENNY:

Without a ball?

GRÜN:

Naturally without one. Ain't that right, Martha?

PETRI:

As you wish, Stephan. (*They pretend to play tennis, imitating* VASCO's *and* MARTHA's *way of talking.* BENNY *laughs*)

GRÜN:

Hurry up and get her for me!

BENNY:

Halfway there. (BENNY *exits*)

GRÜN:

And see that you bring me Mr. Petri's trumpet. You know how helpless he is without music and noise.—You must play with a sweet temper, Martha.

PETRI:

Yes, Stephan! (*Softly*) What's that about the trumpet?

GRÜN:

Backhand, Martha, backhand. (*Softly*) A joke among musicians.—Please, Martha, not into the net, over the net.

VASCO:

She won't be at home.

GRÜN:

Will you be at home, at the hospital?

PETRI:

No, Stephan!

GRÜN:

And why not?

PETRI:

Yes, Stephan.

GRÜN:

No, yes. Is that any answer? Can't ya talk like a human being?

PETRI:

Please, Stephan!

GRÜN:

And now it's please. Just tell me where you'll be.

VASCO:

In any case, not at the hospital.

GRÜN:

Well, where will you be?

PETRI:

With your aunt, Stephan.

GRÜN:

And Benny, where's he running off to, if ya don't mind?

PETRI:

To your aunt, Stephan.

GRÜN:

And who's he gonna find at my aunt's?

PETRI:

Martha, Stephan.

VASCO:

No, no! What's going on? If you're the Chief, what's going on?

GRÜN:

What's going on, Martha?

PETRI:

I don't know, Stephan.

VASCO:

Just chatter back and forth. Am I here to talk about my aunt, talk about Martha?

PETRI:

I don't know, Stephan.

VASCO:

But I know! I'm a cook, and not a speaker.

GRÜN:

Did you hear? Cook, not speaker.

PETRI:

No, Stephan!

VASCO:

Not no, yes, a cook, and I'm going to Schuster and tell him. (VASCO *starts to leave, but* PETRI *seizes him. They throw the pans away*)

PETRI:

Let's leave poor Mr. Schuster out of this. Why, it was just a little joke. Who'd get mad about that? Let's not talk any more about poor Auntie and little Martha, to whom Benny is now running with his swift little feet. That annoys him. Let's talk about something else. Let's talk about his uncle.

GRÜN:

What was his name?

VASCO:

Is no uncle!

PETRI:

Sad world! He denies his uncle.

GRÜN:

He wants to stick him in a dark keg and roll him into the deep cellar. He's a monster!

VASCO:

Well, am I gonna stand here and lie? I'm a cook here. Here I warm up the red cabbage, and soak the kidneys a little. And the laundry, ain't it laying there? Did Mrs. Kühlwasser bring it so we could stand here all dirty? (PETRI *holds him back*)

PETRI:

Do you see a spot?

PETRI:

His *hat* is strikingly clean.

PETRI:

I wonder where he left the old one? (VASCO *starts to leave*)

VASCO:

If ya don't mind, that's enough! What else am I supposed to do?

PETRI:

I'm speechless. Mention the name of your esteemed uncle!

VASCO:

I was talking about my aunt, just about my aunt.

PETRI:

All right, don't cry! Well, what's her name?

VASCO:

Therese.

PETRI:

Aha! Of course, that's not an uncommon name but it's pretty all the same. Wait a minute, who was it had that name?—Somebody or other—never mind. Aunt Therese. —And now your uncle! (PETRI *grabs him*)

VASCO:

I won't say another word!

GRÜN:

That's not supposed to be a vow, I hope.

PETRI:

Maybe he wants to be a saint in a hermitage.

GRÜN:

Or Moltke, the taciturn. Or—now I know . . .

PETRI:

Well?

GRÜN:

He wants a spoonful.

VASCO:

No, no, not that!

PETRI:

But didn't you just now say that not a syllable was gonna get past your lips? And now you do want to tell us your little story? How did it go? A cook ran all alone . . .

VASCO:

We were at my aunt's . . .

PETRI:

That's enough of that! (*They force* VASCO's *arms behind his back*) Stach, come on, my boy!

STACH (*half in front of the wall*):

Something up?

PETRI:

Quick, bring a little spoonful!

STACH:

Jesus, I didn't mean it like that. Believe me, Vasco, I just told what I saw.

VASCO:

You—you claim to be a friend!

PETRI:

Am I gonna have to ask you for two spoonsful?

STACH:

Jesus, right away, Mr. Petri, sir! Just my hands a little, just my hands. (*He dries his hands and vanishes*)

PETRI:

Still not talking? I suppose you'd like to bite your nails. No, no, my little friend. Talking is better.

VASCO:

But the Count didn't say anything. (STACH *comes with the spoon and takes a stance in front of* VASCO)

GRÜN:

So, your little uncle was the Count. Genteel relatives! And what do they talk about in those circles?

STACH:

Well, go on, talk! (*While all stare at* VASCO, THE COUNT *enters right from the kitchen*)

THE COUNT (*laughing*):

Now, now! (*They release* VASCO *and act friendly*) Are you about to feed Vasco? Such a sturdy, healthy fellow?

PETRI:

Just a joke, Count, sir. You know how cooks are. (*To* STACH) Beat it! (STACH *exits behind the wall*)

THE COUNT:

I found out something about them yesterday.

GRÜN:

Something pleasant? (VASCO *withdraws slowly behind the wall*)

THE COUNT:

Depends on how you take it. I thought it amusing.— Vasco! Well, where is he?

PETRI:

Shall I call him?

THE COUNT:

Never mind, Petri. Maybe he's ashamed. The excursion didn't agree with him. Yes, yesterday, at a very late hour, under a very black sky, he made an excursion. Like you, just as you are standing there, covered with a chef's hat that's the very image of yours.

GRÜN:

He's a little peculiar.

THE COUNT:

Grabs me right in the middle of a bridge and wants something from me.

PETRI:

Not money, was it?

THE COUNT:

No, no, no! I don't rightly know what. The girl turned up.

GRÜN:

Martha?

THE COUNT (*pensively*):

I sometimes call her Ruth and see her walking barefoot across a field. It pricks her feet, but she doesn't wince. Were she blind, she would still glean. She is patient.

GRÜN (*as they laugh*):

It almost looks that way.

THE COUNT:

Don't laugh, you idiots! What do you know about patience? Yours would suffice at most for a piece of tough beef, but Ruth . . .

GRÜN:

Let's talk about Martha instead. What happened?

THE COUNT:

She came up, we chatted. What about?—Hm. I don't know any longer. Whatever you talk about on bridges. —Oh, yes, Vasco! He wanted something from me and shook me.

PETRI:

Violently?

THE COUNT:

Like a nut tree. Except that no nuts fell out of my crown. And he wanted to teach me to swim. Me and the recipe.

GRÜN:

Aha!

THE COUNT:

But I see now that you too want . . . you would be just
as . . .

PETRI:

Certainly not, my dear Count! We don't approve of such
methods at all.

THE COUNT:

All right! A suggestion: each of you hold the other's eyes
shut and I'll put it into the pocket of one of you. (GRÜN
and PETRI *hold one another's eyes shut*)

PETRI:

Well, whose?

THE COUNT:

Yours or Grün's.

PETRI:

No, no, no, that won't do it! (THE COUNT *starts to leave*)

GRÜN:

But why not?

PETRI:

I said no! (*He frees himself from* GRÜN'S *hands*) Have
you got it?—The Count! (*With a few leaps they reach
him and drag him back*) Now you just stay a bit longer!
Why won't you tell all of us? To slink away like that!
Aren't we all cooks? It's like a borscht, so it's a cabbage
soup. They say you put ashes in it.

THE COUNT:

That's what you say. But never mind that. I won't give it
to you, you brain-pickers.

GRÜN:

Why the devil not?

THE COUNT:

Because you want to have it, basta!

GRÜN:

But to me . . .

THE COUNT:

Grün doesn't get it either. Sure, I feel sorry for him. He has stomach trouble and he's still a good cook. He's got to cook with his brain and not with his taste . . .

GRÜN:

A good cook . . .

THE COUNT:

. . . never tastes the broth. I know the saying. The wisdom of a man with stomach trouble.

GRÜN:

And Vasco? Does he know, did you give him . . . ? (THE COUNT *retreats*)

PETRI:

You shouldn't have done that. He is your favorite, of course . . .

GRÜN:

Aren't we your friends, too? Why him, him alone?

THE COUNT:

Boys, I'd better be going. You speak of friendship and look at me like brand-new enterprising erasers. Let me live and . . . (*He searches his pockets*)

PETRI:

Are you looking for something?

THE COUNT:

Nothing special, a notation.—What was I saying just now? Oh, yes, let me live.—Gone, vanished!

GRÜN:

Here, in the kitchen? (GRÜN *and* PETRI *get down and search*)

THE COUNT:

It's nothing important, really. Just listen!

GRÜN:

Was it a slip of paper?

THE COUNT:

A little scrap.—You must also let Vasco live, not just me. It's true, he is my favorite, but he knows nothing—just as you know nothing.

PETRI:

Did you find anything, Grün?

GRÜN:

Not a trace. But was it white?

THE COUNT:

As innocence, though somewhat scribbled on. Don't quarrel, boys, if you should find it, and don't mash each other's hats in—they ask for it. (*He taps* GRÜN's *hat lightly and laughing runs off-stage right.* PETRI *and* GRÜN *straighten up.* VASCO *steps before the wall and watches the scene*)

GRÜN:

Why is he laughing?

PETRI:

Because we're sliding around like parquet-layers, looking for a slip of paper which we assume is scribbled on.

VASCO:

And what d'ya think might be on it? He smashes your hats, but ya believe 'im. He calls ya by names, he says "My dear Grün" and "Good old Petri"—then he gets ya on your knees, has a little laugh, and he's gone. He don't even look back. And you? Ya want to give me a spoonful, even two, if ya please, so I'll say something. Well, well, say something. How about it, Mr. Petri? Ya still want to give it to me, huh?

PETRI:

Nonsense, we thought . . .

VASCO:

Well?

PETRI:

. . . you wanted to handle it all by yourself.

VASCO:

Well, I did want to, all by myself, at first. 'Cause he don't

like a mob of people. (STACH *comes in with a bundle*)
Maybe I don't know him? Tell me, don't I know the
Count?

STACH:

I can testify to that. Mr. Petri'll believe me.

VASCO:

He just believes in his spoonful. That's his one and all.
(STACH *throws the bundle between the cooks*)

STACH:

Here's the stuff! She was good and mad, that Mrs. Kühlwasser.

GRÜN:

What about? (*The cooks change aprons and hats*)

STACH:

How should I know? Hasn't she ever been mad before?

GRÜN:

We ought to be nicer to her. We might need her someday.
Send her some of the jellied meat and some other trifle.

PETRI:

I'm still the one who decides what's carried out of the
kitchen here.

STACH:

Jesus, as if Mrs. Kühlwasser wasn't part of the business.

PETRI:

Not another word!—Listen a minute!—If we don't do
something, we're through.—Mr. Schuster said that if we
don't get the place running again in three weeks the way
it was . . . You know what will happen then! And you,
Vasco, don't let it get you down. A stupid, regrettable
mistake. (*He helps him tie his apron*) Grün is always a
little impetuous. Isn't that right, Grün? But it wouldn't
ever have gotten that far.

GRÜN:

We wanted to intimidate you, that's all.

STACH:

I thought, too, that you were only pretending. Would I have brought you the spoon otherwise? (*From the left* BENNY *pushes* MARTHA *into the kitchen. He is carrying the trumpet*)

VASCO:

Oh now look here, have ya got to do that? Nice apologies with nothing to back them up.—She goes right back!

BENNY:

Don't get excited! It was the Chief's orders. The little thing didn't want to come at first, because of your aunt. Here, your megaphone, it's like new again. (*He hands over the trumpet.* PETRI *unwraps it*) Ah, Mrs. Kühlwasser has been here! (*He changes*)

MARTHA:

Stephan?

BENNY:

Isn't that sweet, when she says "Stephan"?

PETRI:

Shut your trap!—She can go again, we don't need her.

MARTHA:

Stephan, your aunt . . . (*He turns his back on her*)

PETRI:

What's wrong with his aunt? Were you inside?

BENNY:

Not a second, Chief. She didn't let me in.

MARTHA:

She's dead. (BENNY *laughs*)

PETRI:

What's so funny? Now leave, girl, go on! Your Stephan will come later and help you. (MARTHA *exits hesitantly*) That's the way it goes. We were just talking about her, and now it's over. (*He blows a note and puts the trumpet on the floor*) The aunt is dead! (*All but* VASCO *laugh*)

STACH:

Go ahead and laugh—as long as she's dead!

VASCO:

Yeah, oh yeah. It's really funny. (*The cooks exit behind the wall laughing. Some dry their hands on the hand towel.* PETRI *holds* STACH *back*)

PETRI:

You, get that chicken ready, and then wrap up some jellied meat with five pieces of pickled pork ribs for Mrs. Kühlwasser. I'll take it to her myself! (*He exits.* STACH *approaches the trumpet, picks it up, turns it this way and that, holds it like a telescope to his eye, and puts it down again*)

STACH:

Music, music! (*He circles around the trumpet and reflects*) The chicken! All right, I'll fix the chicken. We'll see. (*He pulls a meat block from the wings and puts the trumpet on the block*) Music? Music? (*From the left the cook* KLETTERER *enters and watches* STACH *amusedly for a while*)

KLETTERER:

Do you slaughter trumpets at your place now and make trumpet soup?

STACH (*without turning around*):

Jesus, Kletterer!

KLETTERER:

A genteel establishment, I must say! Bright, good ventilation, hardly a kitchen odor—almost like the fresh air of summer.

STACH:

How did you get in here? (*He turns around*) Did he see you?

KLETTERER:

It doesn't look like it. (*He grabs* STACH *by the apron*) How are things going? Did he open up?

STACH:

Just a lot of nonsense. They groveled before him, and he laughed, that fine nobleman, when Grün and Petri crawled around looking for the scrap of paper.—Now get out! If he sees you, all hell will break loose.

KLETTERER:

And what now? (*He takes* PETRI's *trumpet*) Do you have any plans? Is there anything good on the program?

STACH:

Not that I know of. (*He pulls a basket out of the wings. A chicken is moving around in the basket*) Here, I'm supposed to kill a chicken and wrap up some jellied meat and five pieces of pickled pork ribs for Mrs. Kühl-wasser. Petri intends to take it to her in person.

KLETTERER:

What do I care about your jellied meat!

STACH:

So you don't care? Even if Petri takes it to her personally, it's all the same to you?—Ah, now you're beginning to catch on in your midget head.

KLETTERER:

Do you mean . . . ?

STACH:

Big shindig, I tell you. They're going to rent the drying room for the night and have a ball with the Count and all that sort of thing.

KLETTERER (*whistles meaningfully*):
When?

STACH:

Am I a mind reader?

KLETTERER (*grabs* STACH *again*):
But I'll be informed in time, won't I, Stach? You won't be so silly as to spoil your friendship with Kletterer. You know I'd like to be present when you have your party. I love delirious parties!

STACH:

Now stop it! What are you grabbing me for?—They always go for clothes, Vasco, too.—I'll send you a note by pigeon when the moment comes, by carrier pigeon!

KLETTERER:

You know my address! (*Trumpet under his arm, he exits quickly left*)

STACH (*missing the trumpet*):

Music!—Music? (*He sets the basket with the chicken on the meat block, then puts it on the floor again*) Music! Music! (*He imitates the movements of a chicken in front of the basket, tries a handstand in front of the basket in order to look the chicken in the eye, and cackles. He jumps up on his feet, opens the basket, pulls out the wing-flapping chicken and flourishes a knife*) Music! Music!

(*The cook* PETRI *rushes out from behind the wall*)

PETRI:

How often must I tell you, you're not to slaughter chickens right out onstage! Do you want to make vegetarians out of our customers?

CURTAIN

Act IV

(The drying room of a laundry: MRS. KÜHLWASSER *is pull-ing the trousers, aprons, and hats of the cooks on long lines up to the ceiling.* GRÜN *sits writing at a table and supervises her work)*

GRÜN:

You can leave the last row down.

KÜHLWASSER:

What do you need the room for, anyhow? I'm not usu-ally like this, in case you have a meeting. It can even be late, if you let me know ahead of time. But do you have to wake me up, and let's go, let's go, let's go? Is it some-thing special?

GRÜN:

We're celebrating a birthday.

KÜHLWASSER:

Tsk, as if cooks care anything about birthdays. I suppose one of them has done something silly again, eh?

GRÜN:

How long have you been making money off us, any-way? A few years, is that right? Every week, two sets of uniforms, and on top of that, the towels, the linen, and whatever else came along—all white stuff.

KÜHLWASSER:

There's enough to do, I can't complain.

GRÜN:

That's what I wanted to hear. My suggestion is, you don't ask questions!

KÜHLWASSER:

I suppose you'll let me put in one more word.—Tsk, tsk,

249

that Mr. Grün. Sits there and writes. Maybe place cards
or maybe even birthday verses.

GRÜN:

Are you through?

KÜHLWASSER:

It looks like it.

GRÜN:

Then call Martha! (*He points to the door*)

KÜHLWASSER:

Now I'm going to get stuffy. Is it nice to let a body
stand outside in this weather? Doesn't she get enough
with that fellow, what's-his-name?

GRÜN:

Vasco.

KÜHLWASSER:

Now I ask you! And just recently her aunt died.

GRÜN:

It wasn't her aunt.

KÜHLWASSER:

Anyway, that was the only human being she could lean
on, if I may say so.

GRÜN:

You may, Mrs. Kühlwasser—and now! (*He points to the
door*)

KÜHLWASSER:

I'm going, I'm going! (*She opens the door*) Poor thing!
What manners! (*She pulls* MARTHA *inside*) And take that
thing off!

MARTHA:

Yes, Mrs. Kühlwasser. (*She takes off her raincoat*) Good
evening, Mr. Grün.

GRÜN:

Warm up there at the pipes. I don't need you any more,
Mrs. Kühlwasser. And forgive us! This is an exception.

KÜHLWASSER:

I thought you said a birthday.

GRÜN:

That's just it, it doesn't happen often. So, if anyone should ask . . .

KÜHLWASSER:

Then I'll say: That was a birthday party. Is Mr. Schuster coming?

GRÜN:

Probably.

KÜHLWASSER:

Did he accept?

GRÜN:

I said probably. (*He stands up*) We doubled your fee because of the late hour. (*He hands her an envelope and a slip of paper*) There, are you happy now?

KÜHLWASSER:

If it really was a birthday party, of course, I wouldn't say anything.

GRÜN:

Good night, Mrs. Kühlwasser! (*He hands her a second envelope and pushes her to the door*) Sleep well!

KÜHLWASSER:

Take it easy, take it easy! Is this my place, or am I a visitor here? And you just let Martha alone! You watch out, child. Don't put up with anything, if they get fresh. Just keep saying no. After all, they're just little cooks!

MARTHA:

Mrs. Kühlwasser, may I . . . (*She starts after her*)

GRÜN (*pushes* MRS. KÜHLWASSER *out of the room*):

Stay here! Don't be so scared, darling.—So, you were able to get away?

MARTHA:

The head nurse didn't want to at first. But then Dora— she's the night nurse—put in a good word for me.

GRÜN:

That was nice of her.

MARTHA:

We get along fine, Dora and I.

GRÜN (*fumbles at her blouse and* MARTHA *fends him off weakly*):

Well, then. Well, then. So you two get along fine. Does she have a boy friend? (*He grabs her*)

MARTHA:

Please!

GRÜN:

I asked if she has a boy friend!

MARTHA:

I think so. No, please, Mr. Grün! (*She tears herself free*)

GRÜN:

Oh, all right! (*He wipes his hands off on his apron*) What were we talking about? Oh, yes! What is he? Mailman, taxi driver, or maybe a cook?

MARTHA:

What are you thinking of? Do you think all nurses have cooks for boy friends?

GRÜN:

That would be the limit! (*He walks back and forth*) Such a nitwit! So talented! Has the touch! Doesn't have to work at anything! Everything just falls into his lap. And then he goes around with a nurse.—Do you know that you're standing in his way? That young fellow could make a fortune with his talent. But, as I was saying, this relationship! A cook and a nurse: what can that add up to? A mediocre diet kitchen at most. Love is fine and dandy. But not for us. You're standing in his way, my child!— Don't bawl now!

MARTHA:

But he says . . .

GRÜN:

He's a dope. Young, dazzled, he can't do anything about it, only you can. You have to come to a decision. You must say no. You must make the sacrifice. That shouldn't be hard for you, as a nurse. You've all had practice.

MARTHA:

But he isn't *sick.*

GRÜN:

Ah, but he *is!* Mortally, as sure as my name is Grün. That hospital air is corroding him. Chlorine, carbolic acid, aluminum acetate. Have you ever known a cook who could stand that? And always that cap on your head. Your hair will thin and fall out.

MARTHA:

I beg you, Mr. Grün! What am I supposed to say to all this?

GRÜN:

You ought to think it over. very calmly, and at the right moment make a small sacrifice. After all, it's for your Stephan.

MARTHA:

Yes.

GRÜN:

And then you'll . . . (*He listens*) Stop that bawling! (PETRI *enters the room, wearing a black raincoat. He takes the coat off as he enters and tosses it to* MARTHA, *to hang it up*)

PETRI:

Is it going all right? What does Kühlwasser say?

GRÜN:

Gone to bed.

PETRI:

And what else?

GRÜN:

They ought to arrive any minute. Everything's about ready. She was bawling.

PETRI (*he pats* MARTHA):

Okay, okay. It'll be all right. Why is she here, anyhow? Was that necessary?

GRÜN:

I believe so.

PETRI:

Such confused affairs are deeply repugnant to me. I demand the most sparing use of resources and a pure motivation. Won't you explain to me . . .

GRÜN:

She's here and that's that. What about the Chief? Is he coming?

PETRI:

I don't like it at all.

GRÜN:

I asked whether he's coming!

PETRI:

No!

GRÜN:

But he agreed to.

PETRI:

I am not at all pleased. That girl shouldn't be here.

GRÜN:

We ought to be more considerate of each other's feelings.

(PETRI *turns away*)

PETRI:

What a surprise—Grün has feelings.—Mr. Schuster sends word that his presence would be superfluous. He has complete confidence in us and he's thoroughly convinced that we'll be successful in conducting the negotiations in his and our behalf, and without hasty actions of any kind.

GRÜN (*he whistles meaningfully*):

What a philanthropist!

PETRI:

I think you get the idea.

GRÜN:

If only the others understand you. You've forgotten your trumpet. How're you going to make yourself understood without it?

(*The door is flung open.* BENNY, STACH, *and* VASCO, *loaded with packages, push* THE COUNT *into the room. The cooks are wearing raincoats,* THE COUNT *a cloak over his dressing gown.*

THE COUNT:

Petri, Grün! What a surprise! After being torn rudely from sleep and after a not exactly gentle ride, I find friends waiting.—Oh, you here, Miss Martha—at this hour?

VASCO:

Who called her? We didn't agree on that!

PETRI:

My feelings exactly! Calm down, we'll settle that later.— I'd be sorry if these boys gave you a hard time.—Benny!

BENNY:

He didn't want to, Chief.

STACH:

He wanted to go on dreaming.

PETRI:

Apologize, will you!

THE COUNT:

Not at all! Now, since I'm on dry land, as you might say, those small unpleasantnesses are almost forgotten.—I think it's nice here. It doesn't exactly smell good . . .

VASCO:

It smells like cabbage and poor people.

THE COUNT:

You have a sensitive nose. What a shame you're not all nose.—Cabbage, but why not? Purely optically this little room is a feast for the eyes. This mass hanging! What a sight, what a sight!—My dear Grün, does this little picture have some significance perhaps?

GRÜN:

Just a coincidence! The drying room of a laundry. It's warmest up there, and so . . .

THE COUNT:

That reassures me. I was almost crushed by the feeling—the unpleasant feeling—that I was confronted by a symbol or, what's even worse, that I'd have to spend the rest of the night under a symbol.

PETRI:

You can stop worrying, Count, sir.

THE COUNT:

Well, I have to believe you.—And now?

STACH (*softly*):

We'd better get started!

PETRI (*softly*):

What's the matter?

STACH:

They got wind of it and are right behind us.

PETRI:

Damnation! How is that possible? Vasco, Benny?

BENNY:

No idea, Chief. Somebody or other mustn't have kept his mouth shut.

VASCO:

What are ya looking at me for? Wasn't Grün there? Or Stach, he likes to talk.

STACH:

And where were you today at noon?

PETRI (*loudly*):

Quiet!

THE COUNT:

Now, Petri! Let's leave the matter as it is. I assume you

still scold your people. You shouldn't do that in front of a young lady. (*To* MARTHA) I'll anticipate the gentlemen and offer you this chair. (*She sits down timidly*) If Grün —our chief of protocol—will permit me, I'll occasionally sit on the edge of the table.—And now, let's get down to business! Evidently it concerns for the umpteenth time the aforementioned soup . . .

VASCO (*leaps forward*):

Now tell us, at once, I beg you! Or if ya want to give it just to me, why not? Didn't I swear, on my oath, that I'll bury it, here, the recipe in here? (PETRI *jerks* VASCO *back*)

STACH:

Why does he always have to try to get a head start?

PETRI (*softly*):

I warn you, Vasco! (*Aloud*) How nice that you get right down to business. Let's talk like friends. You see, the future of our profession, indeed of all gastronomy, not to mention . . .

THE COUNT:

Humankind.

PETRI:

You said it! You were always a promoter of our difficult but highly important occupation. You always stood by us in deed and word whenever it was a matter of complying with the special wishes of our pampered clientele. But more than that! Generously, you granted us a look at your writings. May all this, your whole collection— the guys brought it right along, though they didn't have to—may it serve as proof of your by now legendary passion. In these packages . . .

THE COUNT:

They probably got damp.

PETRI:

Get going, take them to the radiator! You too, Vasco,

you too! (*They drag the packages to the radiator.* MARTHA *starts to help.* THE COUNT *stops her*)

THE COUNT:

Heavens no, that paper is no concern of yours.—But go on, Petri, I interrupted you. (*There is a violent pounding at the door*) It seems to me the interruptions are just about to begin.

PETRI:

You talk to them. (*Grün gets up and goes to the door*)

GRÜN:

What about? About you? They don't like to talk about our great trumpet impresario. (*He leaves the room*)

PETRI:

Okay, okay.—What were we talking about?

THE COUNT:

About everything on earth, and that paper. You're distracted, overworked. You ought to get some sleep.

PETRI:

Right, the packages! Now, may we assume that perhaps a few notes about the soup, I don't know in which bundle . . .

THE COUNT:

Not at all. You're proceeding on false assumptions. We're not concerned here with just any old recipe, but with my very own wretched little secret. (VASCO *leaps forward*)

VASCO:

That's it exactly, secret!—Can I, Mr. Petri? I've got something to say to him!—What is that, a secret? Is it allowed to remain that—a secret? Will ya die one day and take it with ya? Will ya lie there, and your mouth say nothing more—and here, inside, the secret? (*He strikes himself on the chest*)

THE COUNT (*laughing*):

Your questions are stepping on each other's heels. You're looking in the wrong spot. Not here in my heart! On the street, in a trash can—or sometimes the wretched secret walks about. On three legs, very slowly, like a lame dog, it limps from tree to tree, leaving a dim shadow of its lusterless existence.

(GRÜN *returns and bolts the door*)

BENNY:

I'm going crazy! Now he's going to finish us off!

STACH:

He's pulling our leg. Let Grün speak instead of Petri. Is he going to tell us jokes and sell us a bill of goods?

PETRI:

Quiet!

GRÜN:

They're all here, Petri, every one of them!

PETRI:

Kletterer?

GRÜN:

He's fully informed.

PETRI:

Ridiculous! What can he know?

GRÜN:

Ask him! You're the right one to talk to him. They'll be glad to stand by and listen in to you talking.

PETRI:

Benny, Stach—to the door!

·STACH:

That's useless. If he wants to, he'll come in anyway.

PETRI:

Make it snappy!

STACH:

But Grün ought to talk. He can do it better.

PETRI:

I wonder . . . Well, why not?

GRÜN:

He takes care of me like a father. He'd even give me his

K

shiny trumpet, if only he had it here. (*The cooks laugh*)
And now quick.—Listen! I've dealt with the people outside. They're capable of anything. They don't have our
patience. You don't know them—they won't hesitate. So,
be smart! Here's paper, ink, everything you need. Write,
for Heaven's sake, write and we'll protect you from this
gang.

THE COUNT:

You're poor businessmen—first you get me into a dangerous situation, then you want something in return. You
must make an offer—make an offer!

PETRI:

How much? (*There is violent pounding at the door*)

GRÜN:

Say, those boys are powerful!—He means money. How
much?

THE COUNT:

Your couple of cents, don't make me laugh! (*The pounding increases*) Why not let them in? Those folks are
freezing.

PETRI:

You're very rash!

STACH:

Stop the drivel! He doesn't want money, and he won't
get anything else. What's the use!

THE COUNT:

You ought to know! I want to go home, I must get some
rest. Think it over, decide what you can offer, and
then come back.—Poor Martha! you must be worn out!
(*Pounding*)

STACH:

They're going insane out there!

BENNY:

What a mess! They're letting that fellow take them for a
ride!

STACH:

Not even Grün knows how to handle this. Well, I'd learn him.

BENNY:

Give him a spoonful, if he wants to be offered something!

GRÜN:

Our own people are getting unruly. Go ahead, write!

BENNY:

He can even have two, if he wants. (BENNY *leaves the door. He pulls a bottle and a spoon from his pocket*) How about it? It tastes better cold.

THE COUNT:

Petri, tell your unwashed Benjamin to stand away from my nose! His toothpaste doesn't smell good.

BENNY (*kicks*):

So much for toothpaste, so much for unwashed, and one for your birthday!—How about it—should I . . . (*He looks at the others*)

STACH:

To hell with it! Am I Hercules, that I can keep them off for hours on end? (*The door breaks open with a crash. Several cooks crowd through the opening, the tall cook* KLETTERER *in front. He is holding* PETRI'S *trumpet and blowing on it.* STACH *leaps to one side*)

KLETTERER:

All right, now, let's get going! What's this little game called? May I join in? Speed seems to be wanted. Little spoonful, that's a game we know—it makes you talkative. (*To the rear*) Pipe down, folks, we're in on the game. What's that? (*He points to the packages*)

THE COUNT:

The gentleman refers to my modest collection of recipes.

KLETTERER:

Quiet, back there!—And I suppose you're the modest Count? Kletterer's my name. What, you don't know it? You just wait, we'll be friends!

THE COUNT:

Why not? The best friendships are often made at such a late hour.

KLETTERER:

A comedian!—What about the negotiations? Grün?

PETRI:

Say, Kletterer, where did you get my trumpet?

KLETTERER:

I'm talking to Grün. I was asking about the negotiations.

GRÜN:

Unfortunately, we'll have to adjourn.

KLETTERER:

Nonsense, let me try it! (*He shoves* GRÜN *away from the table*) So, you don't want to?

THE COUNT:

My good man, I want to go to bed, nothing else. And I'm sure the young lady does, too.

KLETTERER:

Lady? Oh, yes, the nurse. So you want to go beddy-bye? Me, too!

(*The cooks in the background become restive*)

GRÜN:

You must make an offer, Kletterer, make an offer! He doesn't want money.

BENNY:

So why not a little spoonful! (KLETTERER *smacks* BENNY *in the face. The cooks in the doorway laugh*)

KLETTERER:

Quiet, dammit! (*To* PETRI) Badly brought up, that fellow. Is that what they learn at your place?

PETRI:

He's a nitwit, what can you do about it?

KLETTERER:

So make an offer, huh? I always have something in reserve. Listen, Count! That first package, what's in it?

THE COUNT:

Fish, I think, venison, poultry, a few sauces.

KLETTERER:

Anything you particularly value?

THE COUNT:

Just stuff I've collected—I thumb through it now and then . . .

KLETTERER (*nudges* BENNY):

To the door with it! (BENNY *drags the package to the door.* KLETTERER's *men rip it apart*) Well, isn't that something! That's the way I'm bidding! Have another?—The next two! (*Two other bundles are ripped apart*)

THE COUNT:

Your performances are somewhat boring, though I must admit that you're saving me a little work. Anyway—one of my little weaknesses—I sort out everything first, save a few things, compare—in short, I make some sort of selection. You and your people are more thorough.

KLETTERER:

You see, boys? We're getting closer. Thoroughness!

THE COUNT:

Avanti! Out with the rest, Benny! You're doing your job well!

KLETTERER:

Wait a minute! I'm giving the orders around here!

PETRI:

But not for long, now. Poor Kletterer! And he enjoys being Chief so much. People like him wear themselves out quickly. (*To* KLETTERER) Well, what else do you have to offer? Your friends aren't at all pleased with you. They're grumbling. You must do something, or they're going to bite your head off.

KLETTERER:

I'm not getting anywhere with him. Let me take a short break.

GRÜN:

Oh, go on, break! Think hard! Maybe we'll play blind-
man's buff or ride piggyback. Maybe we'll consult the
cards and predict a rosy future or . . . (*to* THE COUNT)
. . . let's pull his shirttail out and tickle him a little, our
bashful Count.

THE COUNT (*jumps up*):

Grün!

GRÜN:

What's the matter, what's the matter? Look who's sensitive!

STACH:

What a fright he gets when somebody mentions shirt.—
Maybe he's as handsome as a young god, with a smooth
skin?

BENNY:

Or maybe he's got a couple of pimples somewhere?

STACH:

I wonder whether he has hair on his chest and someplace
else?

BENNY:

And I'd like to know whether he has anything at all!

STACH:

Surely you don't mean . . . ?—That would be terrible!

BENNY:

Take a peep!

STACH:

Then you think the Count can't?

BENNY:

Well, what with?

STACH:

And he pees through a little tube . . .

THE COUNT:

Petri!

STACH:

Well, now, he's yelling for help! Is he getting nervous! Does something go wrong, when his shirt's off? Isn't he the Count any longer, without a shirt?

KLETTERER:

Quiet! Back there, too! How do you mean that, Grün? I don't follow you exactly.

GRÜN:

A little suggestion! You talk to your people, have them go home like good little boys; of course, you stay here. What would we do without you, the big Chief with Petri's little trumpet . . .

KLETTERER:

And then?

GRÜN:

As soon as your boys have disappeared, Vasco will stop biting his nails so voraciously and do a little business with me and the Count. Isn't that right, Vasco? You know how he's got to be talked to.

VASCO:

Now look here—all of a sudden! Why not before? I had to go with Stach, and with Benny there. What does Mr. Petri think I am? A little cook who jumps when somebody says: Run!?

GRÜN:

You have offended him, Petri—say something!

PETRI:

Fine, get him to talk! Do whatever you please.

THE COUNT (excitedly):

Don't allow that, Petri! If Mr. Schuster finds out about it, what is he going to say?

PETRI:

You must see that I'm powerless at the moment.

VASCO (steps forward):

That's it! He can't do a thing without his music. Get your boys away, Kletterer!

KLETTERER (*forces his grumbling people out of the door and locks it*):

Go home! I'll handle this for you. Yes, indeed, I'll keep you informed. I'll be tough, you can depend on it.

VASCO:

How clean the air is all at once, with them gone. Now things will go fast, very fast.

THE COUNT:

What are you planning to do?

VASCO:

Just talk a little about this and that.

THE COUNT:

You won't be able to prove anything. It's all rumors, gossip.

VASCO:

But when did I say what people are talking about? I'm just saying that they're talking. Of course, there's nothing to it, but maybe there's something to it. Our friend, the Count, has no luck with women!

GRÜN:

I don't believe it.

VASCO:

But that's what they say. And the real wicked ones whisper that he loves handsome young men. He even supposedly enticed our tender Benny and laid hands on him.

BENNY:

That's true, I can swear to it!

GRÜN:

Will you please!—Stupid talk and nothing to it!

VASCO:

Grün's right! Sure, we who know the Count say: That couldn't be true! He's a little shy. Whenever he sees Martha coming, he gets red in the face and says: Young lady.—Now I ask ya, what's that? Is it love? Grün,

Kletterer, is it?—Well, all right, and why not? Don't he have reason enough? Don't she come to me, crying and saying: Oh, the Count . . .

MARTHA:

Stephan, I beg you!

VASCO:

Yes, you do! Well, do ya want me to let 'em know everything ya tell me about him? Isn't it my disgrace, if I betray everything? Don't I always ask myself: Why do ya run after Martha, when she's really interested just in the Count? And when she says Stephan, don't it ring in your ear like Herbert?—That's his name. (*To* MARTHA) No, not a word, and don't say my name any more!

PETRI:

Go on, Vasco, go on!

VASCO:

All right, right away.—You're silent, Count, sir. But you're not silent 'cause it ain't true, but 'cause it *is* true, and 'cause I hit where it hurts. Well, let people talk, I thought to myself. Let 'em say the Count hasn't got a heart. I know that he has, and that I hit it. Did I, tell me now, did I?

THE COUNT:

Yes, Vasco, you did. You're an explorer after all.

VASCO (*exhausted*):

Well, all right. I can't go on. You talk, Grün!

MARTHA:

Why are you saying that? Stephan, what have I done to you?

VASCO:

That's over now. Now ya must go to him and call him by name. Go to him—well, go on now!

GRÜN:

I assume that Martha is willing. I had a few words with her before. What did I say, Martha?

MARTHA:

I don't know any longer.

GRÜN:

Forgotten already? Didn't I say: That won't work, a cook and a nurse. Well?

MARTHA:

It was probably something like that.—But you, Count?

THE COUNT:

I can think of nothing, my child. Vasco said it all.

GRÜN:

Enough! The matter is as good as settled. Read that through at your leisure and sign your esteemed name lower left. Would you like to have a chair?

THE COUNT:

Of course not.—You have almost won.

GRÜN:

We have won!

PETRI:

Or even better, you have won, too. Such a splendid girl. Healthy, industrious, patient, never disobedient. You'll be happy, have a fine home, and maybe later on children . . .

THE COUNT:

If Martha wants to come with me. First, just for a time. I have a country house with a garden—she could stay there as a visitor. Let me finish! And then if you all come in a few weeks and she wants to remain with me, not only as a visitor, then I'll give it to you.

GRÜN:

But why not right away? After all, she has already said yes. It couldn't be lovelier in church.

STACH:

That's what I think. Isn't that good enough for him?

BENNY:

He means to put one over on you!

GRÜN:

Vasco, what do you think?

VASCO:

Let 'em go, both of 'em. We'll come out later.

GRÜN:

Kletterer, Petri?

PETRI:

Get it in writing, it's safer.

KLETTERER:

Only if I help write it.

GRÜN:

You can even blow your horn. (*The cooks laugh and draw up a paper.* MARTHA *steps up*)

MARTHA:

Why don't you ask me what I think? I was supposed to be on night duty today. But then they came and got me, and now . . .

THE COUNT:

Would you rather stay with him?

MARTHA:

With Stephan? (*She bends over and picks up some of the scraps of paper*)

THE COUNT:

No, child, let them have the paper. They need it more than you do. (*He goes to the table*) My name? (*He signs*) You have a hurried hand, Vasco. You'll hardly be able to keep up with yourself. (*He goes back to* MARTHA. *Before* PETRI *can grab it,* KLETTERER *takes the paper and looks at it*)

KLETTERER:

I'll take the liberty of watching over this paper, and your highly sensitive instrument as well. Look, there it is! I thought right away he wasn't a count. His name is Schymanski. Herbert Schymanski. (*He sits down and polishes the trumpet*)

THE COUNT:

It must almost be morning.—Martha, you wouldn't mind, would you, if we went and had breakfast now? (*He puts her wrap around her.* GRÜN *hands him his cloak*)

MARTHA:

Stephan, I'm going now! (*They both exit*)

STACH:

A fine couple! (*To* VASCO) Why are you looking after them?

VASCO:

It's gotten light.

STACH:

But you're looking after them as though they were abandoning you. Why?

VASCO:

So they'll think of me. So I'll be like beef stuck in their teeth. (MRS. KÜHLWASSER *enters the room with brooms and a pail*)

KÜHLWASSER:

Well, how was the birthday? It looks quite jolly here. (*She sweeps the recipes to the door and looks at the broken lock*) Say, who's been playing strong man here?

GRÜN:

Never mind, Mrs. Kühlwasser. Take this, have a new one made, but don't talk about it. There's been enough hot air here. It's probably dried that stuff up there.

BENNY:

Why did you all just let 'em go? (*All go to the door*)

STACH:

I don't understand, either.

VASCO:

To give him some time with her, sitting at a table and lying in a bed, now that she's not a nurse any more.

KÜHLWASSER (*lowers the laundry from the ceiling and drapes it over the cooks*):

What ails this character, anyway? He's always biting his nails and planning something for the future.

CURTAIN

Act V

(*The garden: A wall of medium height encloses a garden
and a small country cottage. Left, the garden gate; right,
the gable of the house with windows and a door beneath.
In the garden a few flower beds, a small fountain, a flag-
stone terrace directly in front of the house. A table and
chairs stand on the terrace. The wall is two-thirds white-
washed, the rest dirty gray. Paint bucket and brush lie
on a stool.*

THE COUNT *and* MARTHA *enter through the garden gate.
Both are dressed in light, summery clothes. They are
barefoot, carrying their shoes in their hands*)

THE COUNT (*seizes the brush*):
And now it will get its final brilliance! It ought to look
like a holiday. Innocent and a little boring.

MARTHA (*on the terrace*):
Please, Herbert, not before we eat! How good it feels to
stand on the flagstones!

THE COUNT (*drops the brush and steps onto the terrace*):
The feet are happy, and it cools you up to your ears.

MARTHA:
How dirty your feet are!

THE COUNT:
And yours. Show them to me, child. (*He sets his shoes
and hers on the table. They sit down and he takes her
foot*)

MARTHA:
You mustn't look at them, Herbert. They grew too big.

272

THE COUNT:

They're dusty. And under the dust, reddened and scratched.

MARTHA:

Please!

THE COUNT:

Now let me! I don't know whether they're beautiful, but your feet are good. You should always go barefoot.

MARTHA (*laughing*):

Like your Biblical Ruth, and glean busily at the same time. As though I had nothing else to do but hop over the stubble.—And now they're going to be washed. You ought to wash yours, too.

THE COUNT (*holds her*):

Don't go! Washing feet and finishing the painting of the wall, that can wait.

MARTHA:

And you've put the shoes on the table! What a sight!

THE COUNT:

It looks peaceful, a little weary. (*He mixes the shoes up*) No matter how they lie, they're still our shoes. Even if I look at their soles, and then compare how we've run our heels down.—And you stepped on a beetle—as though you could step on a beetle!

MARTHA:

Take them off the table now, Herbert!

THE COUNT:

And I say leave them there! They've earned it. Other people walk half a mile and bring back a whole bush of wild flowers, then take vases and put flowers and vases on the table. Other shoe-owners come home as though they had a campaign, a raid, a plundering expedition behind them—we bring home our old, good-natured shoes, maybe with some new knots in the shoelaces.

MARTHA:

The way you talk!

THE COUNT:

What? Do you mean our somewhat faded leather flowers couldn't compare to tulips or poppies?—What else can I do? I will have to make vases out of them. (*He picks a few flowers and puts them in the shoes*)

MARTHA (*stands up*):

Fine—let them stay there until later. But then . . .

THE COUNT:

Then you'll come with your checkered tablecloth and the dishes. Then they're supposed to be shoes again, and we in the shoes, as though we'd been born in them. But now you're still the one who walks through stubble, and your feet are so big that you're always a bit ahead of me—even when you go behind me. (*She picks up a bucket*)

MARTHA:

May I say something now?

THE COUNT:

But . . . (*He tries to hold her, but she pulls away from him*)

MARTHA:

No buts. I'm going to the fountain with this bucket (*she fills it at the fountain*) and bring it to you half full.

THE COUNT:

And the goldfish?

MARTHA:

There'll be plenty left for him. No more excuses, no new inventions and flower still-lifes. Your feet are going to be washed.

THE COUNT:

And you, what are you going to do in the meanwhile?

MARTHA:

I'll watch you.

THE COUNT:

And then? (*He washes his feet*)

MARTHA:

Then I'll take a towel and rub them dry for you.

THE COUNT:

And then afterwards, when I bring you a pailful and watch you and start to dry your feet, I'll need two towels and they'll barely dry off just your two littlest toes.

MARTHA:

The way you talk! Everything I have seems large to you.

THE COUNT:

You're a giantess! When I move my hand across your back, I take a long trip. Let's say, from Rome to Copenhagen.

MARTHA:

But before you start off for such distant cities, just let me. I wouldn't want you to catch cold and fall sick before you get there . . . (*He holds out his feet to her and she bends down and dries them*)

THE COUNT (*leans back. The heads of the cooks bob up over the wall*):

It's hot today. I won't paint the wall until after we eat. Don't you think, too, Martha, that it's better that way? (*They both look at the wall, catch sight of the cooks, and give a start*)

STACH:

She's washing his feet and drying them off with tender care.

BENNY:

And then he does the same for her. One little foot washes the other.

STACH:

I call that love!

BENNY:

I wonder whether they're so helpful to one another in

other things! (*They laugh.* KLETTERER, *with a trumpet, jumps onto the wall and runs back and forth, using the trumpet as a telescope*)

KLETTERER:

But the garden does look nice. A bit too many flowers, no vegetables.

BENNY:

You don't understand that. They live on roses.

STACH:

Their menu is something like this: (*He sits down on the wall*) First, pansy soup with primrose on the side.

BENNY:

And then stewed lilies-of-the-valley with purée of violets and forget-me-not filets.

STACH:

To end up with, because it was so good, a little more carnation cheese.

BENNY (*squats on the wall*):

And if they get the tummy-ache, the young vegetarian lovers will have a sip of dewy-fresh dew from the blossom of the bluebell . . .

STACH:

And wash each other's feet with tenderness until lovely love is restored and oh-oh-sweet-sweet and isn't that nice. (STACH *and* BENNY *embrace mincingly.* KLETTERER *blows mournfully on the trumpet*)

KLETTERER:

Say, you! It's really nice out here. It might not be a bad life.

THE COUNT:

Do you like it?

KLETTERER:

Not entirely. I seldom get involved with flowers. How does it go, Benny? What does the poet say?

BENNY:

Let flowers speak!

KLETTERER:

Right! And that's why we're here, too. We want to get the little flowers to speak. (*The three cooks laugh uproariously*)

THE COUNT:

Well, don't squat up there on the wall like ravens that turned out somewhat too pale. Come in, boys, we haven't seen one another for a long time. Vasco, Petri, Grün! Well, why don't you say something?

KLETTERER (*brandishes his trumpet*):

Here's the music. They've nothing else to report. Listen, Count, I'm the Chief now, and when Mr. Schuster wants something, he comes to me and says: "Kletterer, straighten that out, will you? Petri made a terrible mess of it. But I can depend on you, of course, can't I?" And boy! Can he depend on me!

PETRI:

Well, you're a poor speaker, Kletterer, but you have a good physique.

GRÜN:

You mustn't take him so seriously, Count, sir. You know Mr. Schuster: Today this one is Chief, tomorrow somebody else. None of them can blow a trumpet.

STACH:

Petri has been somewhat cut down.

GRÜN:

And Kletterer has become puffed up a bit.

STACH:

Nevertheless, we're all still good friends, Vasco and Grün . . .

GRÜN:

But, naturally, we're not just going to drop old Petri.

STACH:

He's been somewhat cut down, though. What does that mean, anyway? Who can tell me who'll be the big man tomorrow?

KLETTERER:

It certainly won't be you!

STACH:

Who knows? Who knows? (VASCO *sits down on the wall*)

VASCO:

What a sight she is! No longer a nurse. And she's fixed her hair now so that ya can see it all the time. I would never have thought Martha was that blonde!

PETRI:

Do you hear that love-talk? Any minute and he'll get himself a guitar and rhapsodize about his lost happiness.

VASCO:

I always thought she didn't have a neck, and now she has one. And the way she moves her hands, like she could work wonders with them, like every finger had a special touch and knew where the very spot was in her partner.

PETRI:

How is it all going to end? Do something, Kletterer! Show us what you can do!

GRÜN:

You're too strict, Petri! He's been in charge only a little while.

STACH:

He's got to get the hang of it.

GRÜN:

We ought to help him.

KLETTERER:

I don't give a hoot for your help! It's going to go fast now. Are you all ready? Hup! (*Trumpet sound.* BENNY *and* STACH *leap from the wall, and* THE COUNT *stands up*)

THE COUNT:

They're stepping on everything! Can't you come through the gate, you dimwits?

BENNY:

Did he say dimwits?

STACH:

He thinks we're still the Benny and the Stach we used to be.

THE COUNT:

Now they're stomping down the borders. Call your boys out of the garden, Petri! (PETRI *points at* KLETTERER) All right, then, Kletterer!

KLETTERER:

You misjudge the situation. We were invited here, so to speak.

BENNY:

We've been here three times already.

STACH:

And always the bird had flown.

THE COUNT:

I repeat my request. Call your people back!

KLETTERER (*Trumpet sound*):

Everybody halt! Countermarch! March! Hm! They don't obey me any more. I wonder if it's the trumpet? (*He inspects the trumpet*)

BENNY:

Let's begin! (*He pulls a slip of paper from his pocket*) Here, read it through, write legibly, or better still, print. (*He starts to lay the paper on the table*) That looks cheerful! Shoes on the table! Whose boats are those?

MARTHA:

Mine, Benny.

BENNY:

Tsk, tsk! I suppose he's not talking to me any more. And that stuff there?

MARTHA:

The flowers? Oh, just a game.

BENNY:

If it isn't another trick!

STACH:

Let them have their little game. Do we have time to talk about trifles? We've been here three times, and all for nothing. And you talk about games!

BENNY:

I just want to have room. (*He sweeps the shoes off the table and lays the paper on it*) We must have order.

THE COUNT:

It's senseless, Kletterer! I won't negotiate with these fellows.

KLETTERER:

But why the devil not? It doesn't matter, does it, who brings the papers? (GRÜN *and* PETRI *laugh*)

PETRI:

That's just the way I thought it'd be!

GRÜN:

Kletterer had an idea. He wanted to send Benny and somebody else. So that they could talk to the Count.— Common people.

KLETTERER:

But . . .

PETRI:

That was a flop!—Grün, you take care of the matter! (*He climbs up on the wall.* GRÜN *disappears behind the wall and enters through the garden gate*)

KLETTERER:

All right, if that's what you want. I like to be surprised.

BENNY:

They just want to intimidate you, man. We'll manage it.

KLETTERER:

I told Grün, basta! Go on to the gate! Stach, too!

STACH:

Jesus, he sure wants to show that he's still the Chief. (*They both take up positions at the garden gate*)

GRÜN:

If you will allow me, Count, sir—and pardon the way these guys are acting. Let's make it short, as usual. Our last agreement, you remember, in writing—see, your firm, strong signature right here. No chance of a mis-understanding, a signature like that speaks volumes, the signature of a man of high intellectual stature.

THE COUNT:

You all want the recipe.—I'm sorry.

KLETTERER (*leaps from the wall*):

Who's sorry here for what?

THE COUNT:

I've told all of you often enough, it is not a recipe, it's an experience, a living knowledge, continuous change— you ought to be aware that no cook has ever succeeded in cooking the same soup twice.

KLETTERER:

All well and good. But what are you sorry about?

THE COUNT:

So I have to be more explicit. The last few months, this life with Martha, with my wife—all right, my dear, may I say that?

KLETTERER:

What about your life here?

THE COUNT:

It has made this experience superfluous. I have forgot-ten it.

KLETTERER:

The recipe? You don't mean to say that . . .

THE COUNT:

I would gladly have helped you. To explain precisely: even after the first few days together, probably even after the first few hours . . . how was it, anyway, my dear?

MARTHA:

We went to your place, you cooked us breakfast . . .

THE COUNT:

. . . and you asked if you could put two lumps of sugar in your coffee.

KLETTERER:

My, you have an astonishing memory!

THE COUNT:

I remember everything very clearly.

KLETTERER:

But not the recipe, huh?

THE COUNT:

I never thought of it again—until now.

MARTHA:

I thought of it. I have dreaded this day.

KLETTERER:

You have every reason to, young lady, and your phony Count, too. I'm gonna, I'm gonna . . . (*He seizes him*)

PETRI:

What are you going to do, Kletterer, huh? (*He climbs down from the wall ceremoniously*) What super-sly ideas have you got in your nursery noggin now? You notorious inventor of fried potatoes, you gruel-dabbler, you casserole genius!

KLETTERER:

I'll make him talk, and her, too!

PETRI:

No, no, my dear fellow, that's not the way. Frankly, you lack kindness.

GRÜN:

Let him do it! Don't make such a fuss! After all, nobody said that you're not the Chief any longer.

PETRI:

I even let him have my trumpet! Look at it! Dull, dented, no proper care. What do you say about that, my dear Count? Is that the way to treat a valuable instrument?

THE COUNT:

You should have hidden it better.

PETRI (*laughing*):

Should have hidden it! Did you hear that? Advice—he, he gives me advice; he, the man of mystery, the man of forgetfulness! (*Seriously*) Now you just listen to me! We've known each other for quite a long while. You realize that I've been responsible for the gentle tone of our negotiations up to now. (*He screams*) But I can change!

THE COUNT:

We're afraid so.

PETRI:

Both of you! Now don't think all that puts me in a gentle mood: that almost-white wall, flowers in front of it, and this ridiculous fountain.—Benny, what's that little fish called?

BENNY:

I'll just ask it. (*He fishes in the fountain and hands* PETRI *the captured goldfish*)

PETRI:

Here, you probably know him! A minute ago he was cheerful, now he's gasping for air. He doesn't like it at all that you still won't tell us your little story. And he won't like what I'm going to do to him now, either. Very carefully, I'll stick him in my pocket and give him a pat or two. Maybe he'll tell me the recipe. Well?

THE COUNT:

I wonder if that little fish deserves your displeasure? Punish *me*, Petri! Something will occur to you, but leave this little life in the fountain. Your relations with trout, pike, and tench may be excellent, but certainly you're not up to a goldfish.

PETRI:

Stop talking, man. It brings out my true nature. You see, I'm finally catching on to your methods. Take that former nurse by the arm, go into the house, and consider it—think about it! Then we'll come and ask again, very briefly, you understand! And then you'll moan—no, the two of you'll cry out: Petri, Petri, oh, that Petri!

THE COUNT:

And you, Vasco? What do you say? You're sitting on the wall.

VASCO:

I look at her, but she don't look at me any more, and she don't say Stephan to me, either. (*To* MARTHA) What's the matter with ya, anyway?

MARTHA:

Let's go, please. It's gotten chilly in the garden.

THE COUNT:

Right away, my dear. Too bad! I would like to have finished painting the wall. Maybe you'll do it, if you have the chance, Vasco. It doesn't look right, unfinished like that. (THE COUNT *and* MARTHA *exit into the house*)

VASCO:

He wants me to! All right, why not? He has her, has Martha, and I paint the wall for him.

KLETTERER:

And the recipe?

PETRI:

Piece by piece, I'll get everything out of him.

GRÜN:

Are you so sure? He'd tell us, if he knew it. He doesn't have any reason to keep secrets any more. He has what he wants.

STACH:

The Count would never lie. But we can't admit it, and say there's nothing to be done. We must act as if he still knows, and finish it, so that there's an end to it.

PETRI:

But you're talking complete nonsense! He doesn't want to, he still wants to put us off. Maybe . . .

VASCO:

No maybe! The Count says what's what. Ya want to go up there and take what he don't have? Ya want to go up the steps and get rough and ask him, Where's the soup, what makes it gray? And how much ashes and what kinda ashes to make it gray, and then start all over again? Why, how much, and what kind of ashes? Ya want to ask like that?—Hand the shoes up to me, Benny!—Well, d'ya want to be like the can opener that don't know what it's doing? Ya want to stand there like Rasputin and make a gloomy face and act like you're sinister?—Just give me the shoes, the big ones!

PETRI:

Go ahead, hand them up to him!—You know him, Vasco. Speak up.

VASCO:

What shoes Martha has! And with worn heels.

PETRI:

And if he does know something, after all?

VASCO:

All right, you're the smarties. Ya know how to fix it so that anybody tells what he knows. But if he don't know any longer, I ask ya! If there was that eraser—love—and it rubbed out everything in his mind, and in his heart, and he don't know anything any more. How many ashes, what kind of ashes, and when ashes?—I'll take 'em to the shoemaker for her, and buy her some shoelaces. (*He loosens the old shoelaces with his teeth*)

KLETTERER:

Maybe he's remembering again.

GRÜN:

Such a thing takes time. There wouldn't be any sense now in making him . . .

PETRI:

Oh, go on! He'll always say: I don't know.

VASCO:

What's always? Is always eternity? Is that a thing they sell in church with songs and sweet smells? Boy, are we smart! (*He stands up on the wall*) When did the Count know? Well, when did he know the details, and since when don't he know any longer?—Boy, what knots she has in her shoelaces! (GRÜN *and* STACH *laugh*)

STACH:

That Vasco, the things he thinks of!

GRÜN:

Squats on the wall and longs for his Martha.

STACH:

Unties knots in the shoelaces with his gnawed-on finger-nails and with his teeth, and thinks and thinks.

KLETTERER:

Like a kid! Does he want the nurse back again?

GRÜN:

Our short-term Chief is kind of slow to catch on. Explain it to him, Stach!

STACH:

Jesus! If innocence had its seat in the brain, he'd be a virgin and wouldn't know a thing. What is there to explain? Vasco gets Martha back and the Count recalls what love made him forget. (STACH *and* BENNY *join hands and dance*)

STACH *and* BENNY:

> Dollar, dollar, you must wander
> From this place to that out yonder.
> Oh, how wonderful, how droll,
> See the dollar roll and roll.

(VASCO *shows signs of restlessness*)

PETRI:

Quiet! What's the matter, Vasco?

VASCO:

But if she don't want to, 'cause, 'cause, well, 'cause . . .

PETRI:

Did she *want* to go with him before? Well, then?

GRÜN:

Maybe he'll be quite happy to be by himself a bit again. Basically he doesn't care much about women.

BENNY:

Then he can finish painting his wall in peace and quiet.

VASCO:

He did say he'd like to have painted it all white.

(*Two pistol shots ring out close together. The window shutters above the door spring open.* VASCO *stiffens and drops* MARTHA'S *shoes, one after the other*)

STACH:

Now why is he shooting?

GRÜN:

Now Vasco will have to finish painting the wall.

(VASCO *stares into the open window*)

STACH:

What's the matter, what are you listening for? Did he shoot you, too?

PETRI:

Vasco! (*Slowly* VASCO *turns to the cooks*)

VASCO:

The recipe!

KLETTERER:

What about it?

STACH:

He knows it! I can tell by looking at him. He caught on to something!

VASCO:

No, no!

BENNY:

We'll see about that.

(KLETTERER, STACH, *and* BENNY *dash to the wall and climb over.* VASCO *jumps backward from the wall*)

VASCO:

I won't tell ya anything, not anything!

KLETTERER, STACH, *and* BENNY:

Vasco! Vasco! He's running to the left, there, next to the slope, and now he's behind it. He wants to climb up on the tracks . . . the tracks!

VASCO (*from the distance*):

No, no, no! (PETRI *and* GRÜN *peer, listening, after them*)

PETRI (*raises the trumpet and tries to blow*):

Not a sound! Uh-huh, uh-huh!—There they go! Do you know why?

GRÜN:

It has something to do with legs.

PETRI:

And the recipe?

GRÜN:

An excuse for running. Nobody wants it any more. It's not a matter of the soup, of course.

PETRI:

And why don't we run?

GRÜN:

Let's wait a little while. When those fellows get tired and want some new, rested-up shoes, then—well, we'll have to exert ourselves some.

PETRI:

Good old Vasco! Only he won't have any time to go to the shoemaker. He'll have to tramp around restless and barefoot.

GRÜN:

He won't even have a second left to bite his nails. And he did like to do that so much!

PETRI (*takes the goldfish from his pocket*):

I wonder if he'll also be as mute and stingy with words as this luxury article, this ornamental fish. (*He tosses it into the basin*)

GRÜN:

Well, the owner of this fountain attraction had a few things in common with all finny creatures. His fish dishes were justly famous.

PETRI (*at the edge of the fountain*):

He's turning up his belly. He doesn't care any more.

GRÜN:

And neither you nor I—nor anybody who wields a spoon and is paid as a cook, nobody can force him to be a goldfish again and swim off. (PETRI *polishes the trumpet*) I don't like it here any more! (*He exits running*)

PETRI:

There he goes! But in my legs, too, something is getting ready to strike out for a hypothetical goal! (*He hurries his stride and finally exits running*)

27

CURTAIN

3.4.74